DANTE'S LYRIC POETRY

Dante's Lyric Poetry

K. FOSTER AND P. BOYDE

Volume I

THE POEMS

TEXT AND TRANSLATION

OXFORD

At the Clarendon Press

1967

Oxford University Press, Ely House, London W.1

GLASGOW NEW YORK TORONTO MELBOURNE WELLINGTON
CAPE TOWN SALISBURY IBADAN NAIROBI LUSAKA ADDIS ABABA
BOMBAY CALCUTTA MADRAS KARACHI LAHORE DACCA
KUALA LUMPUR HONG KONG TOKYO

PRINTED IN GREAT BRITAIN

CONTENTS

v

CONTENTS

CONTENTS

vii

CONTENTS

INTRODUCTION

WE do not know in what year Dante began the *Divine Comedy*, but we can be fairly sure that it was after all or almost all the rest of his verse, the *Rime* assembled and annotated here, had been written. The last of the poems in this volume, *Amor, da che convien*, was very probably composed in 1307–8 when Dante was a little past forty. The earliest of them he wrote in his teens. A little more than twenty years separate the first sonnets with their conventional rhetoric and pretentious obscurity from the splendid intellectual and technical assurance of such poems as *Tre donne* and *Doglia mi reca*, both written, it seems, between 1303 and 1305. The *Comedy* was yet to come but already at the opening of the fourteenth century Dante was easily the foremost poet writing in Italian; and he was also, as the *De vulgari eloquentia* (1304–5) was soon to show, the one with by far the clearest understanding of the historical situation of poetry in that young language and of its relation to poetry written in the other Romance tongues, especially Provençal. He was, in fact, a major critic as well as a great poet. A similar combination of talents is found, of course, in other major poets—Goethe and Leopardi, Coleridge and Eliot are names that come to mind—but there are two reasons for stressing its special importance in Dante. The first is the extent to which his own poetry is the result of critical deliberation, of a conscious reflection on questions of technique; and in what follows a good deal of stress will be laid on this point. The other reason can only be touched on in passing here: it is the importance that attaches to his critical reflections from the fact that they occurred just when they did. When Dante began to write and reflect on poetry, Italian literature was hardly more than half a century old; it was linguistically uncertain, very limited in scope and range, and still largely overshadowed by French and Provençal, to say nothing of the massive cultural and linguistic background represented by Latin. When Dante died in 1321, not only had he written in Italian the greatest single poem ever written in a Romance language, but he had critically explored in all directions the situation in which a writer in Italian actually found himself at that particular time. He had squarely faced the alternative of Latin or vernacular and decided, triumphantly, for the latter. He had explored the problem—to be sure, without, as a critic, satisfactorily resolving it—posed for the Italian poet by the variety of Italian dialects. He had mapped out the history of the Italian lyric through the thirteenth century, and done it with so firm a hand that the outline he imposed on the material has, broadly speaking, been accepted ever since.

But Dante was of course a poet first, and only secondarily a scholar or a critic; and if he studied poetry it was only, or chiefly, in order to make it. He never said anything very deep or original about poetry as such, considered speculatively. What he does say—not only in his Latin book on vernacular 'eloquence' but intermittently also in the *Rime* and the *Comedy*—is a great deal about the art of verse, in particular about the elements that come together in a poem and compose, so to say, its body: the aural effect of words, the structure of period and stanza, rhyme, etc. This did not exclude—far from it—a belief in 'inspiration', in the possibility of the mind's being roused and strengthened by superhuman influences— though the Muses, by the way, never appear in Dante's verse before the *Comedy*, nor is their special role filled in the *Rime* (except in no. 89, lines 1–10) by the omnipresent

Amore. In a general way Dante believed in a *Verbum aspirans de celis* (*DVE* I. 1) just as he believed in natural predispositions to poetry (*ingenium*, 'ingegno') on the human side (cf. *DVE* II. iv. 9; *Par.* XXII. 112–14). But it is not on these 'given' factors that he lays his stress, but rather on such as come from discipline and hard work—on systematic knowledge, *scientia*, and acquired skill, *ars*; and especially on *ars*, which for Dante meant any kind of skill that had been or could be reduced to a set of rules, a technique. As an art, poetry too must have its rules and technique, and it is under this aspect that Dante habitually considers it, stressing as a matter of course its formal, constructive side—whether explicitly, when speaking as a teacher of rhetoric, as in *De vulgari eloquentia* II, or implicitly, when speaking through his poems. All this was inevitable, given his cultural background. And all this, it need hardly be said, would have little interest for most of us today if it had not played an essential part in the writing of great poetry. Only scholars and historians can be expected to take much interest in medieval rhetoric as such, apart from its embodiment in the work of genuine poets.

It has already been implied that Dante had no general theory of poetry that could properly be called philosophical. In this he was like other men of his time. Medieval thought, as Curtius remarked, 'produced no aesthetics and no theory of art', at least as we understand these things: if in our century a Maritain has succeeded in formulating a Thomist aesthetic,[1] he has done so only by combining and developing insights and distinctions that were never drawn into a system by St. Thomas or by any of his contemporaries—taking the notion of beauty from brief definitions which placed it on the

[1] *Art et scolastique*, Paris, 1927 (2nd ed.); *Creative Intuition in Art and Poetry*, London, 1954.

border-line between the more closely studied concepts of *verum* and *bonum*, and the notion of art from the scholastic psychology of 'habits', which in effect did little more than define art as the 'intellectual virtue' concerned with making, *recta ratio factibilium*—an excellent definition so far as it goes, but one which obviously says nothing specific about the fine arts or poetry. To get closer to an idea of poetry the medievals invariably—before Petrarch at least —turned back to the pre-philosophical disciplines which were the basis of their education, the seven so-called Liberal Arts grouped into the *trivium* and *quadrivium*. We see Dante do this, for example, when commenting on his own canzone *Voi che 'ntendendo* (no. 59) in *Convivio* II. xi. Having distinguished the meaning, *sentenza*, of a poem from its beauty, *bellezza*, with the implication that the former is wholly convertible into prose, he then analyses the beauty—the formal aspect in virtue of which the poem *is* a poem—into three components taken respectively from three of the Liberal Arts: grammar and rhetoric (which belonged to the *trivium*) and music (contained in the *quadrivium*). As we shall see, these three 'arts' enter into the making of a poem in different ways and with different relations to the final result; but the point to note here is that Dante was content with this very simple analysis—with conceiving the beauty of a poem as merely the effect of skilfully applying rules drawn from those three 'arts'. It would be interesting to compare him on this matter with Petrarch; for Petrarch was later to show himself decidedly reluctant to reduce poetry to a product of the seven Arts; like philosophy itself, it transcended them all (*Invective contra medicum*, III). And no doubt Dante too would have admitted, in some sense, poetry's eventual 'transcendence' with respect to the 'arts' from which it derived; but he never discussed the point, and if we seek some more general notion with which to connect his idea of poetry, we have to turn to the traditional notion of eloquence, *eloquentia*.

This term, in the whole Latin tradition from Cicero onwards, of course included prose as well as verse—indeed in the first place it had been applied to prose (oratory) and only later by extension to verse. But by Dante's time this extension was traditional, as we see from the way he alludes to poets as *vulgares eloquentes* or *eloquentes indigenae*, or to the poet Sordello as *tantus eloquentie vir* (*DVE* I. x. 3; xii. 9; xv. 2). But though in this way a rather general term, *eloquentia* was not, in the Latin and medieval tradition, at all vague. It presupposed, to start with, a twofold distinction: between men and brute animals, and between educated men and the uneducated. Man is distinguished from the brutes by the gift of speech; an educated man is distinguished from his fellows by the fact that in him this gift is cultivated, so that he can aptly and easily express whatever he thinks and feels; which is precisely to be eloquent (compare on these points Cicero's *De Oratore* I. viii with the twelfth-century humanist John of Salisbury's *Metalogicus* I. i–vii). A whole cultural ideal is thus implied in *eloquentia*, an ideal which it was the special business of the 'masters' of the Arts of the *trivium*—grammar, rhetoric, and logic—to maintain and transmit. But the connexion was closest between eloquence and rhetoric; hence poetry as a type of eloquence came under the government of rhetoric. And two further points should be borne in mind here, in approaching Dante's poetry. First, the traditional and classical distinction between the mere gift of speech and its product, ordinary speaking (*loquela, locutio*), on the one hand, and cultivated speech (*eloquentia*) on the other, led in medieval pedagogy and literary practice to a certain association of true 'eloquence' with the *evidently* artificial—with forms of expression that visibly departed from everyday colloquial forms or a logical structure. Thus a chief mark of an educated, that is, a rhetorically trained man's style was that it was *ornatus*, 'decorated'. When Beatrice sends Virgil to help Dante it is on his 'parola ornata' that she relies, and the phrase is almost equivalent here (*Inf.* II. 67) to 'poetry'. The 'decoration' could take many forms according to an author's subject-matter and purpose, but in general the studied avoidance of everyday speech that it implies is a fairly constant feature of medieval writing, except (and it is admittedly a large exception) where the author's aim is purely didactic as in the prose of scholastic philosophers and theologians. The reader will find a great deal of 'ornamento de le parole' (*Con.* II. xi. 4) in this sense in Dante's *Rime*.

The other point to bear in mind, arising from the close connexion between poetry and rhetoric, is that the medieval poet very commonly addressed himself to a definite and stated audience. Many poems were, of course, written in the form of soliloquies, but on the whole it was more usual then than it has been for the last two centuries, for poems to take the form of an address to a person or persons. In Dante's case it is rather exceptional to find him *not* addressing anyone in a poem: the bulk of the *Rime* is made up of poems explicitly addressed either to another man, commonly a fellow poet (nos. 1–5, 7, 15, 72–74, 75, 76, 84–88), or to a woman (9, 13, 21–23, 27–28, 31, 51–52, 54, 65), or to a more or less definite group of men or women, or both (6, 10, 11, 17, 33, 35–36, 38–39, 47, 48, 56, 57, 83), or to personifications, the most usual being Love, or supernatural beings (8, 12, 18, 19, 24, 59, 62–63, 67, 79, 82, 89), and this without counting the addresses to the poem itself in the *congedo* of most of the canzoni, or the passages of direct speech in the relatively few 'soliloquy poems' (e.g. nos.

16, 20, 32, 40). This preponderance in the *Rime* of *addressed* discourse gave, it need hardly be said, great scope for rhetorical devices and procedures. To take only one example from the love-poetry, the rhetorician's *captatio benevolentiae* is evident in stanza 1 of no. 33; while in moral-didactic poems such as 69, 70, and 83 the whole structure and movement is oratorical, all is aimed at either teaching and persuasion. Considered from this (very relevant) rhetorical point of view a good many of the *Rime* can be read as attempts to fulfil two at least of the three aims which St. Augustine had set before the *eloquens* in Book IV of *De doctrina christiana*: 'ita dicere [debet] eloquentem, ut *doceat*, ut *delectet*, ut *flectat*' (c. 12). For where Dante is not actually teaching (as he clearly sometimes is) he is frequently aiming to persuade (*ut flectat*) as well as to please (*ut delectet*).

Nevertheless the pleasure-giving motive is fundamental in poetry as Dante conceives it; and this because the special function of a poet is to create verbal objects that are beautiful. Beauty, in Dante's view, is the least you can expect from a poet, for it is precisely what he is equipped to provide. Thus he makes his canzone *Voi che 'ntendendo* say to the reader: 'If you cannot grasp my meaning, at least consider my beauty.' The meaning could be set out in prose, as in fact it is set out in *Con.* II; but in writing this exposition Dante was conscious that he was leaving the beauty behind—in the poem where it belonged. And that it does belong there, and what it consists in there, becomes clear enough if we turn to the passage in that prose commentary which has already been referred to—the analysis of poetic beauty into elements drawn from grammar, rhetoric, and music: from grammar the construction of the sentence, from rhetoric the 'order' of the poem as a complete discourse, from music 'the number of its parts'. 'Number', 'lo numero', refers here of course to the interrelation of units of sound to form a rhythm, the arrangement of words in a metrical pattern; in the context it denotes precisely what makes the canzone a poem at all. This exists as poetry in so far as a grammatically and rhetorically well-ordered discourse has been shaped into a metrical pattern and so received a special additional beauty. Prose can be beautiful (cf. *Con.* I. x. 12–13; *DVE* II. vi) but good verse as such is more so, since beauty consists essentially in a perceptible harmony and correspondence of parts in a whole; and where such parts are words it is the special effect of the poet's 'musical' art, by inter-linking or, to use Dante's term, 'binding' words together, to give them all the harmony, and therefore beauty, of which they are capable. The basic idea connecting beauty with poetry— and with music—is that of the interrelation of parts in a whole. We call a thing beautiful, says Dante, 'cui le parti debitamente si rispondono, per che de la loro armonia resulta piacimento' (*Con.* I. v. 13). Now the art which *par excellence* aims at and achieves such harmonious interrelation is music, 'la quale è tutta relativa, sì come si vede ne le parole armonizzate e ne li canti, de' quali tanto più dolce armonia resulta, quanto più la relazione è bella' (*Con.* II. xiii. 23). So far then as words become, in this sense, musical, they become beautiful; and it is the poet above all who can give them this beauty, because in his art—and his alone—the art of music is conjoined with the arts of rhetoric and grammar.

Thus the poet, for Dante, is a musician with words; his special effect on them is a 'legame musaico'. Poets are defined as 'those who make harmony with words', *armonizantes verba* (*DVE* II. viii. 5—where the poet is perhaps distinguished from the musician proper by a light stress on the noun *verba*). A naïve etymology is brought in (as so often in medieval writers) to support this favourite idea: the word 'autore', author, says Dante, derives in one of its senses from the Latin *avieo* (a form of *vieo*) 'to bind together', and in this sense the term is applied only to poets, for they are those who bind words together with the 'art of the Muses', 'con l'arte musaica' (*Con.* IV. vi. 3–4). It is true that in the only formal definition Dante offers of poetry he may seem to lay an equal stress on a specific *content* and on the purely rhetorical element, where he calls poetry *fictio rethorica musicaque poita* (*DVE* II. iv. 2), which we might render: 'a product of imagination expressed with the aid of rhetoric and music'.[1] But the general drift, without doubt, of Dante's scattered allusions to the art of poetry is towards identifying its specific element with music, taking this term in the special sense it has in this context —the art of treating words as items in an aural harmony. Prose can embody a *fictio*, and good prose is shaped by rhetoric (cf. *DVE* I. x. 2; II. vi), but no prose can bring out the latent interrelations and harmonies of words to anything like the extent that verse can. Such harmonies are the proper concern of the poet. To avoid misunderstanding it should be added that for Dante the musical quality, the harmony and consequently the beauty of verse is not exclusively the effect of conjoining smooth or 'sweet' sound-items. It is so where the poet's style is 'dolce'; but there was also the 'stile aspro', the harsh style, which Dante began to develop in the mid 1290s (see especially no. 80 below) and was to take to its limits in the later cantos of the *Inferno*; there can be no doubt that he thought such poems or passages beautiful and therefore, in their own way, 'musical'.

---

[1] See G. Paparelli, 'Fictio. La definizione dantesca della poesia, *Filologia romanza*, vii, 1960, pp. 1–83; cf. A. Schiaffini, 'Poesis e Poeta in Dante', *Studia philologica et litteraria in honorem L. Spitzer*. Berne, 1958, pp. 579–89.

So, in general, the stress, when Dante is discussing poetry, falls on form and structure, in particular on sound-structure. And this, as we have seen, means that the poet has an overriding concern with beauty. He is a maker of beautiful objects; not *only* this, but very definitely this. His motive in 'making' is what we should now call aesthetic; and in Dante himself such a motive was obviously very powerful indeed, and powerful all through his career. But it combined, of course, with other non-aesthetic motives which (setting aside that of mere vanity) can be roughly classified as moral, political, and religious. On the whole these emerge more clearly in his later poetry, as his powers matured and his human interests widened and he increasingly committed himself to public causes. But it is important to note the intensity of both motives in him—their intensity and their interpenetration; as Gianfranco Contini has said, the 'serietà terribile' of Dante the artist is virtually indistinguishable from a striving for all-round human excellence, from 'l'ansia di perfezione'. To a degree very unusual among artists, these two motives, the aesthetic and the non-aesthetic, were harmoniously related in him. Though he often speaks like an unhappy man, as a poet he must have been singularly happy; his passionate delight in form and construction was only matched by his passionate interest in an immense range of possible themes. The development of his genius was essentially towards the achievement of an ideal balance between the aesthetic and the non-aesthetic sides of human nature; and he stands pretty high, to say the least, among those who have aimed at that ideal.

His growth towards some approximation to it can best be studied in the *Rime*. In the prose works, except perhaps in the *Vita Nuova*, the aesthetic motive and interest are less directly engaged; while the *Comedy* represents of course the term of the growth rather than its process. The *Rime* show us precisely the process—the gradual movement of a superbly gifted but also very alertly self-critical artist towards the mastery of his craft, a movement which was at the same time a progressive assimilation of ever fresh materials. We watch Dante growing, and also watching his own growth with the conscious lucidity that was so characteristic of his procedures. He always wanted to know exactly what he was doing and why. And sooner or later he always wanted others to know too. With all his intense individuality Dante had a very strong sense of the human community, of the interdependence of human minds; for him, to live humanly was to seek reasons for living, and to seek them with others, in a common pursuit, through the interchange of ideas. In a deep sense he did not believe in 'private thoughts'; every thought had a public importance, though the public it concerned might be a small one. The public addressed in the early lyrics is very small— all included, one might say, in line 1 of the first sonnet of the *Vita Nuova* (no. 6 below): 'A ciascun'alma presa e gentil core': it is the rather self-conscious elite of the Italian followers of the Provençal troubadours, either love-poets themselves, or simply interested in 'versi d'amore' because interested in the 'courtly' eroticism that was those poets' conventional theme. Nor did this circle —the circle Dante wrote for—widen at all numerically as he came under the influence, successively, of Cavalcanti and Guinizzelli, and helped to create the 'stil novo', that 'new style' which was to receive the special imprint of his personality in the 'praise-poems' of the *Vita Nuova* (see nos. 33, 35, 43-44 below). The only perceptible change, as regards the public Dante addresses in his 'stil novo' phase, is that we now have an impression of a group of people more closely connected with one another through sharing the same ideas about poetry and cultivating a common style in writing it—or, in the case of the ladies concerned, a common taste, we must presume, in reading or listening to it (see the notes on no. 33 especially). Reading the *Vita Nuova* (the work which *inter alia* traces, explains, and justifies Dante's evolution to his own form of 'stilnovismo'), one is always aware that the author is writing for a 'set' with a common mind and common assumptions, literary as well as moral. In this sense it is an esoteric work. The author does not at all expect—or desire—to be understood by the 'ordinary reader'. Nevertheless, within the small circle addressed by the book the utmost lucidity was expected, for the 'stilnovisti' were true thirteenth-century intellectuals and their mode of discourse reflected the scholastic culture of that time, with its insistence on analysis and ratiocination. It is in the esoteric *Vita Nuova* (xxv. 10) that we are told that a poet should be ashamed of himself if he cannot, when asked, break his poem down into intelligible propositions. And Dante adds that he and his friend Cavalcanti could mention names in this connexion. . . .

It was not, apparently, until he was nearly thirty that Dante began to address a public beyond the small literary circles already mentioned. The external event that led to this change—to judge from his own statements in the *Convivio* (see the Appendix to the next volume)—was the death of Beatrice, the 'gentilissima', in 1290. Her death led, on the one hand, to her apotheosis in the *Vita Nuova* (1292–4), the work that resumes and concludes the first main stage in Dante's poetic career; and on the other hand to the beginning of Dante's serious studies in philosophy and science. He began these studies, he tells us, to console himself for his loss; he continued because he was fascinated by what they revealed to him. And they were to have profound and lasting effects on his poetry. The first effect—again, to judge from his own account (*Con.* II. ii, xii)—was allegory; Dante began to represent philosophy as a 'donna gentile', a noble lady, this image serving for a time as a bridge between his usual earlier theme of refined erotic love and the new themes suggested by his studies; and also as a sort of concession to his usual readers. The next step was to discard the veil of allegory, and this he did in the canzone on Nobility (no. 69), and less drastically in that on 'Leggiadria' (no. 70). It was a risky step to take; but there were illustrious precedents already in Italian, and among them one which must have counted for much with Dante, the rigorously 'philosophical' canzone about love by his friend Cavalcanti, *Donna me prega*. But the point to note here is the widening of Dante's audience, as well as of his interests, that this advance into philosophical (ethical) poetry at least potentially implied: one can hardly suppose that *Le dolci rime* (no. 69) with its deliberately plain style and close reasoning was not intended to interest almost any contemporary Aristotelian who was prepared to read verse from time to time; while its companion piece, no. 70, seems to envisage much the same audience as that for which the *Convivio*, a decade later, was to provide 'popular' instruction in philosophy: 'principi, baroni, cavalieri, e molt'altra nobile gente, non solamente maschi ma femmine, che sono molti e molte in questa lingua, volgari, e non litterati' (*Con.* I. ix. 5). Here of course trained philosophers are precisely those for whom Dante is *not* writing, since he insists that he writes for those who cannot read Latin, the normal language of medieval philosophy. Nevertheless he is clearly now addressing a wider public than he had done in the *Vita Nuova*, though this too was written in Italian; and a similar difference can be felt, though less obviously, between the canzone on 'Leggiadria' and the *Vita Nuova*. There is nothing esoteric about the canzone; when Dante wrote it he was already moving out of the rather closed world of the 'fedeli d'Amore' with its privately shared assumptions and conscious exclusiveness. He was, in fact, growing up. It is relevant to note that his intellectual growth through the 1290s went hand in hand, after 1295, with the increasing engagement in political life which led to his holding the office of a Prior of the Florentine republic in 1300, and then, of course, to his exile from the city. And politics combine with moral philosophy to form the stuff of the two greatest poems of Dante's first years in exile: *Tre donne* (no. 81) and *Doglia mi reca* (no. 83). Obviously, these poems were not aimed at so large a public as the *Divine Comedy* was to be; but the chief factors that would make for the extraordinarily wide appeal of Dante's masterpiece were already present, or emerging, at this time: the factor of the exile itself, with the great enlargement of experience that it entailed; the poet's intense interest in general human problems, moral, political, scientific, religious; his delight in the use of the vernacular, the speech of the 'non litterati', and his growing confidence in its capacity to express the full range of human experience—a delight and a confidence that remained marvellously unaffected by the great cargo of Latin culture, both scholastic and classical, which he was steadily taking on board. From another point of view this extending of Dante's aim, as he grew older, to wider circles of readers went with an extension of his poetry's emotional range. Sexual love, however refined, is a more private emotion than the passion for moral ideals like justice and liberality, or political ideals like the union of the human race under a single emperor, or religious ideals like the reform of the Bride of Christ. Dante's growth as a poet can be seen, in part, as a growing capacity to express the more public emotions. It comes indeed as something of a surprise that his last canzone, the 'Montanina', *Amor, da che convien* (no. 89) should be, in this sense, 'private'.

With this growth, both intensive and extensive, in the power to communicate through poetry, went a constant desire to communicate through critical and expository prose *about* that poetry. Few poets have been so eager to talk about their own work; perhaps, paradoxically, because few poets have been less tempted to complacency. Indeed, it is fairly clear that this eagerness came in part from Dante's acute sense of the limits of human speech (see, e.g., *Con.* III. iii–iv) and so of the inevitable limitations of any given form of speech. Verse could do what prose could not, but the converse was also true; and it seems probable that Dante's almost exasperated sense of the limitations of his media was an unconscious factor leading to the alternations of verse and prose in his work. If the *Rime* as a whole point onwards to the *Comedy* and in a sense (as trials and experiments) only receive their final justification in it, particular groups within the *Rime* find successive provisional issues and justifications in the *Vita Nuova*, the *Convivio*, and the *De vulgari*. Note that these prose works together represent the only attempt Dante himself made to organize and unify the *Rime*. These were never intended to form a single book reflecting the successive stages of one prolonged life-experience, as the lyrics of Petrarch for example were; which is why, incidentally, the title *Canzoniere*, which may suit Petrarch's lyrical output, is quite unsuited to Dante's; for this was written without any single plan and reflects no unity save that of the poet's prodigiously versatile and inventive spirit. But a certain *post factum* organization and grouping was imposed on them, successively, by Dante's recurrent need to stand back and take stock, to justify and explain.

Thus the *Vita Nuova*, under one of its aspects, records and justifies (in terms of a form of loving that required its own appropriate expression) a strictly literary experience, the discovery of the 'praise-style', 'lo stilo de la loda' (c. xxvi); while under another it serves as context and pretext for the young poet's discreet 'placing' of his own work in relation to both the past (the Romance lyric 'in lingua d'*oco* e in quella di *sì*', c. xxv) and the present (represented most conspicuously by Guido Cavalcanti, 'questo mio primo amico', c. xxv, and cf. iii, xxiv, xxx). Thus too the *Convivio*, besides containing the first important defence of the vernacular in Italian, gives the poet's explanation of the decisive new turn that his poetry took in the early 1290's as a result of his study of philosophy—an explanation which entailed not only a detailed exposition of the content of certain poems (nos. 59, 61, and 69 below) but also comments on the allegorical mode of the first two of these, and on a change of style (from 'dolce' to 'aspro') occasioned by the content and purpose of the third.[1] Or again, there is the valuable distinction between a poem's 'goodness' and 'beauty', and the remarks on the use of the *congedo* (II. xi).

But it is in the *De vulgari* that Dante is most concerned with literary criticism as we understand it. The whole argument of the treatise as it stands, in its unfinished state, converges on vernacular poetry considered at the highest level, as an art of writing 'greatly' about 'great' subjects. It states Dante's highest hopes and strictest requirements for vernacular poetry, as these appeared to him in the middle of the first decade of the fourteenth century, when he had not yet begun the *Comedy* but had already in fact written nearly all his *Rime*. So all those hopes and

---

[1] It may be questioned however whether no. 69 really is 'aspro', in the full sense in which no. 80 is 'aspro'. See the notes below on both these poems.

requirements are stated in terms relating to the canzone, which he saw as the form best suited to the grand manner in vernacular verse, to the 'tragic' style as he called it—tacitly assuming that 'greatness' in poetry was all a matter of writing excellently in that style. This matter of style is discussed in Book II, the first seven chapters of which lay down general rules and conditions for the 'best' use (in poetry) of the 'best' Italian vernacular (*vulgare illustre*). Such use should not be attempted except by men who not only have natural talent (*ingenium*) but also minds enriched by systematic knowledge (*habitus scientiae*) and a taste trained by continual exercise in the poetic craft (*artis assiduitas*). Moreover it requires the 'best' subject-matters, and these are identified—by an argument which we need not reproduce here—with War, Love, and Virtue (c. ii). To treat 'greatly' of these 'greatest' topics calls in turn for an appropriate style; and here Dante applies to vernacular poetry the traditional classical distinction of the three styles: high, middle, and low; the 'high' style—*superior stilus*, or as Dante prefers to call it, *tragicus*—being the one required; for which the appropriate metrical form is the canzone (cc. iii–iv). The next three chapters (v–vii) describe the 'high' style in general terms, as applied to verse in the vernacular; and so conclude that section of the whole treatise—namely II. i–vii—which may appropriately be called Dante's Rhetoric for poets in the vernacular. The next six chapters (viii–xiii), being entirely a detailed study of the metrical structure of the canzone, fall under the 'art' of Music, giving this term the sense already explained above. But Rhetoric, the study of style, and Music, the study of metric, both presuppose Grammar, the study of language itself. Hence Book II of the *De vulgari* had to be preceded by the considerations in Book I on the nature and history of language in general (cc. i–viii) and on Italian in particular (ix–xix). Thus the whole of Book I is *prolegomena* to the strictly literary considerations of Book II. The famous survey of the Italian dialects in I. x–xv is only incidentally of strictly linguistic interest; for the 'best' Italian which it aims at identifying, far from being found in the actual speech of any city or region, is explicitly located only in certain literary texts, which are presented precisely as literary models—located in the work of a definite series of poets, starting with those of the Sicilian court of Frederick II and terminating with Cino da Pistoia and Dante himself. Thus by the end of Book I attention is already focused on the language of poetry, and in Book II this theme fans out to become a detailed and very technical exposition of the 'best' poetic form, the canzone. The *De vulgari* was in fact the natural outcome, given Dante's mentality, of his intense cultivation of the canzone form during the 1290's and on into the first years of his exile. As an historico-critical review of the actual situation of Italian poetry, it concentrates on what most interested Dante himself, the development of the canzone from its Provençal origins to its full flowering, as he thought, in his own poetry of the decade and a half preceding, and in the love-poetry of his friend Cino.

It seems appropriate at this point to touch briefly on two further questions suggested by the *De vulgari*. (*a*) How far does Dante's actual practice in the *Rime* conform to the threefold style-division laid down in Book II, c. iv of the treatise? (*b*) How far does that practice conform to the principle, asserted in the same chapter, that vernacular poets ought closely to imitate classical (Latin) authors: *quantum illos proximius imitemur, tantum rectius poetemur* (II. iv. 3)? With regard to both matters we may well feel that Dante's practice was somewhat inconsistent with his theory; and with regard to the first in particular, that his lyrical output shows in fact a freedom and variety which his doctrine does not allow for.

But here we may remind ourselves that the practice of a medieval vernacular poet was naturally conditioned by the vernacular he used, and that for literary purposes this was a relatively new language; whereas medieval poetical theory stemmed from an ancient and very conservative rhetorical tradition. The medieval *Poetriae* ('Arts of Poetry') drew their general rules and principles from such works as Horace's *Ars Poetica* and the *Rhetorica ad Herennium*, then attributed to Cicero; as Curtius said, they 'represent a new adaptation of antique rhetoric'; and what was new in most of them was not directly related to the novelties arising in vernacular literature. This was not, of course, the case with the *De vulgari*, which, as we have seen, owed its *raison d'être* precisely to recent developments in the Italian lyric; while it owes its enduring freshness to the mind of the genius who, with those developments in mind, gave to his own vernacular at once a *grammatica*, a *rhetorica*, and a *musica* built up entirely from first principles. On the other hand, it certainly draws on traditional rhetoric, and nowhere more clearly than in the theory of the three styles, 'high', 'middle', and 'low'. But in the *De vulgari* this traditional, originally classical division serves a very special purpose: it is brought in as a step in Dante's argument to show that vernacular verse could be written in the high 'tragic' style; and he naturally found the pre-eminent vernacular examples of such a style in the Provençal *canso* and the Italian canzone. Hence the argument led him greatly to stress—and from the point of view of his own practice somewhat to over-stress—the particular metrical form, that of the canzone, which seemed most clearly to justify the general conclusion; with the result that he made of a given metrical form as such an essential element in style; declaring that the 'high' style in vernacular verse *required* the canzone form, and that ballatas and sonnets as such were necessarily 'middle' or 'low' (*DVE* II. iii. 2–9; iv. 1, 6; xiii. 1). Now this scheme, though broadly true, is too abstract to fit the *Rime* in every case: metrical form apart, there is nothing to distinguish clearly the style—the diction, phrasing, and general tone—of a ballata such as no. 64 from some of the canzoni; or the sonnets for the 'donna gentile', nos. 51–54, from the first canzone for the same lady, no. 59; or again the sonnet no. 82 from other poems which Dante certainly considered stylistically 'high'. Such inconsistencies between theory and practice are due to his making metrical differences correspond too rigidly to the scheme of the triple style-division.

On the other hand everything in the *Rime* is consistent with the general idea presupposed by that division and underlying all the crucial first four chapters of Book II of Dante's treatise, the concept of literary *convenientia*, 'appropriateness'. This idea—also derived, of course, from classical rhetoric—was one which the medieval mind, so profoundly attached to the idea of order, found perfectly congenial; it expressed in the field of human art the overriding belief that the cosmos was a hierarchy in which everything, from the material elements to the angels, had its proper place according to its degree of perfection—or, as Dante liked to say, nobility. One effect indeed of this stress on an objective order in things may have been the unconscious reinterpretation of the classical doctrine of the three styles which became usual in the Middle Ages (see E. Faral, *Les arts poétiques du XIIᵉ et du XIIIᵉ siècle*, Paris, 1958, pp. 86–89[1]): whereas in classical rhetoric the distinction of styles was chiefly one between modes of expression, in medieval rhetoric the emphasis

---

[1] See now F. Quadlbauer, *Die antike Theorie der 'genera dicendi' im lateinischen Mittelalter*, Vienna, 1962.

came to be placed on diverse degrees of 'nobility' in subject matter: the three *genera* of style—the *grave*, the *mediocre*, and the *humile*—are so called, says the thirteenth-century rhetorician Geoffrey of Vinsauf, *ratione personarum vel rerum de quibus fit tractatus*. There were different styles in poetry, not simply because there were different things to write about, but because these things were more or less important or 'noble' (cf. *Purg.* ix. 70–72). It is true that a poet's choice of a style might depend also on subjective factors: thus the very noble 'matter' which Dante takes up in the first of the 'praise-poems' for Beatrice, no. 33 (cf. *VN* xvii–xix) will be treated, he tells us in the first stanza of this canzone, not 'altamente' but—out of modesty—'leggeramente'.[1] Thus the poet's tone and attitude is a constant factor giving variety to his style whatever the objective 'matter' may be. Hence it is often not possible to place a poem of Dante's with certainty in a given style-category. Some are undeniably 'low' (e.g. nos. 72–74), some undeniably 'high' (81 and 83), some seem 'middle-to-high' (33), some perhaps 'middle-to-low' (43 and 44). What can be stated with certainty is that almost every poem is stylistically consistent in itself, is a stylistic unity. This is not, of course, true of the *Comedy* as a whole, which includes every variety of style of which Dante was capable; not, however, mixed and jumbled together, but used alternately with a strict attention to changes in subject-matter and the effect intended by the poet at any given point in his narrative.

The precept, quoted above from *De vulgari* ii. iv. 3, about imitating classical authors is certainly puzzling at

---

[1] It will be suggested, however, in the notes on this poem, that Dante's 'modesty' here is merely rhetorical—a 'modesty-formula'; cf. E. R. Curtius, *European Literature and the Latin Middle Ages*, London, 1953, pp. 407–13.

first sight; for the plain fact is that there is scarcely anything in the *Rime* that would strike a modern reader as
derived by imitation from any classical poet, Virgil
included. In this respect the *Rime* are utterly different
from the *Comedy*. It is clear that the *Comedy* as a work of
art stands in a very close relation indeed to classical
Latin poetry—to Ovid and Statius, and above all of
course to Virgil. It goes without saying that one cannot call this relation 'imitation' without a good deal of
refining on the word to make it suit so subtle and so
unusual a case of literary dependence. Dante's 'imitation'
of Virgil in the *Comedy* was a vast creative trans-
figuration of Virgilian themes and images and stylistic
devices, which presupposed a thorough assimilation
of the one poet by the other—the 'lungo studio e 'l
grande amore', in fact, which Dante declares to Virgil
in *Inf.* I. 83–84. Of such assimilation there is no
sign in the *Rime*; so that if one were to allow that they
'imitate' in any sense Virgil or other classical poets, one
could only do so by giving this term not more—as in
the case of the *Comedy*—but far less meaning than it usually bears. In the *Comedy* we have, after all, unquestion-
able evidence of how classical influences affected Dante's
poetry; and two effects of that influence may serve to
show, by contrast, how 'unclassical' the *Rime* as a whole
are. The *Comedy* is rich in similes; there are very few
in the *Rime*. The *Comedy* is thickly interwoven with
allusions to Graeco-Roman history, legend, and mytho-
logy; in all the *Rime* such allusions can literally be
counted on the fingers of one hand. What then did
Dante mean by the precept about imitation cited above,
with its implication—surely—that he had himself obeyed
it in the *Rime*? Still more, what did he mean by telling
Virgil, on first encountering him in the *Comedy*: 'Tu se'
lo mio maestro e 'l mio autore; / tu se' solo colui da cu'

io tolsi / lo bello stilo che m'ha fatto onore' (*Inf.* 1. 85–
87)? For only the *Rime* had so far brought him 'honour'.

Anything like a full exegesis of these texts would out-
run the limits of this introduction; it will be enough to bear
in mind the following points. First, as to the *De vulgari* text
—*quantum proximius imitemur*, etc.—Dante himself provides, implicitly, a useful gloss on it in a later chapter
(II. vi) where he discusses types of sentence-structure, *constructio*. After distinguishing four types, graded upwards
from the least to the most rhetorically elaborate, and
declaring that the last is the one used, and rightly used,
by the 'illustrious poets'—that is, those who have written
in the high 'tragic' style—he then mentions no less than
eleven canzoni which exemplify it. Then, and only then,
does he relate these vernacular achievements to classical
Latin models, and he does so in terms which indicate
a generally beneficent influence rather than any imitation
in detail; an influence, moreover, which is not stated as
having in fact operated on the writers of the canzoni just
mentioned, but is merely recommended, and in a rather
surprisingly modest way : 'And perhaps (*fortassis*) it would
be most useful, for acquiring the habit of it (the best
constructio), to have read the "regular" (i.e. Latin) poets,
namely Virgil, Ovid . . . Statius, and Lucan, and also the
best prose-writers, as Livy, Pliny, Frontinus, Orosius. . . .'
This passage, it is clear, enables us to take the precept *quantum proximius imitemur* in a somewhat qualified
sense. In effect Dante is saying: 'the classics are our
examples, not in the sense that we should copy them in
detail, but that they show us in general what beauty of
style can be'.

As for the assertion in *Inf.* 1 implying that the 'bello
stilo' of the *Rime*—or more precisely no doubt, that of
some of the canzoni—had been 'taken' from Virgil, it is
permissible to take this *cum grano salis*, or at any rate in

a decidedly qualified sense. It has been noted that the *Rime* simply do not show the sort of close literary relationship to Virgil's poetry that is evident in the *Comedy*. And biographical considerations tend to confirm this negative conclusion, strongly suggesting that before 1300, the fictitious date of *Inf.* I, Dante had not yet studied the whole of the *Aeneid* in detail. He tells us himself in *Con.* II. xii, that when he began to read Boethius and Cicero in 1292–3, he found them difficult; he implies indeed that he knew some Latin then, but the terms he uses would be very strange if at that time he had been Latinist enough to have already assimilated the *Aeneid*; yet by 1293–4 he had certainly written nearly sixty of the eighty-nine poems of his *Rime*, and some of them in a style which he certainly considered 'bello', if he could cite them as examples in the *De vulgari* (no. 33 in II. viii. 8; no. 40 in II. xi. 8) or recall them with pride in the *Comedy* (no. 33 in *Purg.* XXIV. 51; no. 59 in *Par.* VIII. 37; no. 61 in *Purg.* II. 112). Again, it has been shown (by U. Leo in *Mediaeval Studies*, Toronto, xii, 1951, pp. 41–64) that the first positive evidence of Dante's having read *Aeneid* V–XII occurs only in the fourth Book of the *Convivio*, written in 1306–8. What we know in fact of Dante's studies prior to his exile from Florence in 1302 gives no grounds for believing that they included any extensive attention to Virgil, or for that matter to any classical author. The learning which he acquired in the 1290s, so far as its sources can be identified, was scholastic rather than classical. So far as the *Rime* are concerned there is no doubt at all that metrical forms, language, style, and themes were derived in the first place from Dante's vernacular predecessors and contemporaries. These were the chief immediate models and sources of influence. But these models were impregnated with certain assumptions about expressive speech, with a certain 'rhetoric'; assumptions which Dante must have fairly soon mastered for himself at the theoretical level as well as in the practice of his art, becoming a *rhetoricus* as well as a *dictator*. He assimilated, in short, the Latin rhetorical tradition, and so began to draw near to the classical models and masters always venerated and cited in it. And in due time he came to read those masters *in extenso* for himself. But this close contact with the Latin classics came at a relatively late stage in his poetic career: it preceded, and profoundly influenced, the *Comedy*; it had comparatively little to do with the *Rime*.

In effect, though no doubt this was not Dante's intention, the *De vulgari* is a sort of epilogue to the poetry of his youth and young manhood. It virtually marks the end of the first of the two periods into which his poetic career falls: that of the *Rime* and that of the *Comedy*. In the former period he never stretched his powers beyond the construction of canzoni; these represented the formal limits of his art; but by 1304–5, the date of the *De vulgari*, all but one (no. 89) of his canzoni had been written. And although in the treatise Dante's enthusiasm for the canzone form seems unbounded, the fact is that between the time when he left it unfinished—breaking off in mid sentence in II. xiv—and that of his beginning the *Comedy*, there was probably an interval of at least four years during which his energies went almost entirely into writing prose—into the *Convivio*, which he was still writing in 1308, and into the political Epistles occasioned by the Italian expedition of the Emperor Henry VII. This is to say that between, roughly, Dante's thirty-ninth and forty-fourth years he was far more concerned with criticism and philosophy and political polemic than with creating new poetry. And in so far as he does concern himself with poetry during this interval, he seems on the whole to be looking backwards, not forwards: the

'Montanina' canzone itself (no. 89), though a powerful and moving poem, is in some respects curiously 'archaic'; the *De vulgari*, as we have seen, concentrates on the 'tragic' style of poems already written, while the *Convivio* is an exposition of the content of three of these same poems. In these prose works there is never a hint of any conscious preparation for the *Divine Comedy* (as on the other hand there may possibly be at the end of the *Vita Nuova*), nor any suggestion that the thought of writing major poetry in any form other than the canzone had yet crossed Dante's mind—though an approach to such a conception may perhaps be discerned in his tendency to write *sequences* of canzoni, such as the three commented on in the *Convivio*, nos. 59, 61, 69 (to which may be added 70 and perhaps 67 and 68) or the 'rime petrose', nos. 77–80. It is as though for the time being Dante had pretty well worked through the possibilities which this form offered him; and that the impulse, whatever it was, which would eventually set him to work on the *Comedy* had not yet come.

When that impulse came it was strong enough to set all his powers working together at poetry, and keep them steadily so, with only marginal distractions into prose of any kind. The critic and philosopher was absorbed by the poet; but the poet remained what he had always been, and the new poem, the final masterpiece, itself repeatedly exemplifies that 'constant', as Contini calls it, of Dante's personality: the perpetual 'overtaking' of his poetry by 'reflection on technique', the continual association of 'concreto poetare' with 'intelligenza stilistica'. The *Comedy* itself, notes the same critic, is 'una somma stilistica'; and this without the slightest loss of 'ricchezza vitale'. But it is more to the point here to note how Dante's alertness to his own procedures in the *Comedy* recalls his earlier efforts, and those of his masters and friends, to create an Italian poetic language that would not be too miserably inadequate to the variety and richness, the heights and the depths of human experience. The very professions of verbal inadequacy which have—as of course they were intended to have—such expressive force at certain key-points in the *Comedy*—notably in *Inf.* XXXII. 1–12 and throughout *Paradiso* XXXIII—recall a constant, if unobtrusive, theme of Dante's love-poetry in 'the style of praise': the 'ineffability' of beauty (cf. nos. 35. 12–14; 44. 12–14; above all 61. 1–18, with the philosophical commentary in *Con.* III. ii–iii). Again, that same passage from *Inf.* XXXII, prefacing the description of lowest Hell and declaring the poet's need of 'rime' sufficiently 'aspre e chiocce', cannot but remind a reader acquainted with Dante's earlier poetry of certain adumbrations there of the terrible Dantean 'harsh style'—notably in the sonnet-exchange with Forese (nos. 72–74*a*) and the 'rime petrose' (77–80); adumbrations which already represented a major technical achievement, as the poet of the *Inferno* was perfectly aware, for all his seeming so grandly to discount it ('S'io avessi . . . ma perch'io non l'abbo'). On the other hand the famous reply to Bonagiunta in *Purgatorio* XXIV. 52–54, points to the opposite extreme in Dante's stylistic range, to the 'stil dolce' or 'soave'; and explicitly it relates this style to the first canzone of the *Vita Nuova* (no. 33 below) as to a pre-eminent and permanent model. Or again, the final praise of Beatrice's beauty in *Par.* XXX. 19–33 recalls all the earlier poetry inspired by it: 'Dal primo giorno ch'i' vidi il suo viso / in questa vita, infino a questa vista, / non m'è il seguire al mio canto preciso. . . .'

These examples indicate lines along which one might proceed to study the continuity of Dante's poetry, from the *Rime* to the *Comedy*. That continuity was not least evident in the continued progress and development:

enough to recall, in respect of stylistic development, the virtually new assimilation of classical and Virgilian models referred to above; and in respect of theme and content, the vast appropriation of Christian 'matter' hitherto almost absent from Dante's verse. This double development made the *Comedy* possible; and with it the fulfilment of potentialities discernible, in the light of the *Comedy*, in the minor works, and in the *Rime* especially. It goes without saying that the masterpiece could not have been written had Dante not trained himself so persistently— and inventively—in verse technique; and it is no less obvious that it could not have been written if the technical experimentation, which is so marked a feature of the *Rime*, had not stemmed from the same driving need to represent reality through words as that which later found fulfilment in the *Comedy*. This is only to say that the *Rime* as a whole are the work of a genius in process of discovering his own powers and needs. And that they are the product of genius appears not so much in the technical and thematic variety they display as in the sheer poetic force with which the various themes are handled and the technical resources deployed. Dante did not invent the metres he used; nor was he the first Italian poet to extend the range of vernacular verse beyond the limits of the usual erotic theme. He was simply the first to show a truly outstanding capacity to organize whatever theme he chose into compelling poetic discourse. He combined an astonishing constructive, 'architectural' power with an exquisite sensibility to the sheer expressive quality of words. These two aspects of Dante's genius are not always, one need hardly say, equally in evidence in the *Rime*; now one, now the other, at times predominates. But his innate tendency was towards a poetry whose beauty would be a product of both, a harmony of reason and sensibility, each extended to its utmost; a beauty therefore which would at least in part reflect those outshinings of the divine Goodness, in the sensible world and in the mind itself, which Dante thought it the proper business of the human spirit to consider, record, and imitate.

The present standard text of the *Rime* is that prepared by Michele Barbi for the edition of the *Opere di Dante* sponsored by the Società Dantesca Italiana (Florence, 1921; reprinted 1960). A new, critical edition, by Domenico De Robertis, has been announced, but at the time of writing it is still in the preparatory stages.

Barbi's edition comprises, together with the poems which he attributes with certainty to Dante, twenty-nine other poems by various authors, included because they seemed to be more or less closely connected with Dante's. Of these additional pieces we have retained eighteen in this volume; these being, with one exception, either 'letter-poems' addressed to Dante, to which his own reply is extant, or replies to similar 'letters' by him; the exception is Cecco Angiolieri's sonnet (no. 57a) commenting on the last poem of the *Vita Nuova*, which seemed too interesting to be omitted. For the text of all Dante's poems, and all but two of the companion pieces by other poets, we have followed Barbi's edition;[1] except that we have occasionally modified the punctuation or preferred a different division of words (e.g. *serra* for *s'erra* in no. 4. 5, or *per che* for *perché* in no. 70. 27): these few variants are discussed in the notes. The two poems for whose text we do not depend on Barbi are those by Cavalcanti, nos. 6a and 15a, which are printed as they appear in the critical edition by Guido Favati (*Guido Cavalcanti. Rime,*

[1] For the *Vita Nuova* poems and nos. 72–74 we have, however, followed Barbi's later editions; and in nos. 59, 61, 69 we have taken account of Vandelli's readings.

Milan–Naples, 1957). Barbi's 'Appendice' of twenty-six poems, the attribution of which to Dante he considered doubtful, has been entirely omitted from the present volume. This has seemed the wiser course to follow, pending the appearance of a full discussion of the matter in the expected critical edition.

Textually then the present edition hardly differs from Barbi's. In two other matters we have allowed ourselves more independence. The first concerns the attribution of the poems in the longest of the three sonnet-exchanges between Dante Alighieri and Dante da Maiano (nos. 2–4 below; XLI–XLV in Barbi's numbering). Here, for reasons given in the commentary (see the introductory note ad loc.), we have ventured to reverse the attributions made by Barbi and commonly accepted by later editors; thus we attribute—with, we hope, a proper diffidence—nos. XLI, XLIII, and XLV to Alighieri, and only nos. XLII and XLIV to the other Dante; with the consequence, that in this edition eighty-nine poems appear as by Dante Alighieri, as against eighty-eight in Barbi's edition.

The other matter is the ordering of the poems. In Barbi's edition these are divided into seven books, the first of which comprises only the poems contained in the *Vita Nuova* and some of the companion pieces not by Dante. Abandoning Barbi's division into books, we saw no reason to keep the *Vita Nuova* poems separate from the rest; we have therefore interspersed them with other of Dante's *juvenilia*, the 'Altre rime del tempo della *Vita Nuova*' which comprise Barbi's Book II. This entailed, of course, abandoning Barbi's numbering, and also a reconsideration of the ordering of those 'altre rime'— though not, be it noted, of the *Vita Nuova* poems, which appear here in the order given them by Dante himself (as do the three canzoni, nos. 59, 61, and 69, around which he composed his *Convivio*). Our aim in general has naturally been to arrange the poems in a plausible chronological sequence; basing our decision on considerations of style, theme, and tone, where external evidence is lacking, as it often is. In fact, however, we have largely retained the ordering of Barbi's Book II; the chief exceptions being our 'earlier' placing of his nos. LXII and LXVIII (in our numbering, 7 and 25 respectively).

As to the order of poems in Barbi's Books III–VII, two alterations introduced in this volume should be mentioned here, ignoring some minor transpositions. First: taking as a firm starting-point for Dante's development after the *Vita Nuova* the canzone *Voi che 'ntendendo* (Barbi's no. LXXIX), we have made this the first of an unbroken series of poems (nos. 59–68; in Barbi's ordering, nos. LXXIX–LXXXI, LXXXIV–LXXXV, LXXXVII–XCI), all certainly written before Dante's exile, all love-poems or about love, all characterized by the use of a broadly similar 'sweet' style ('stil dolce'), and all more or less open to the kind of allegorical interpretation which Dante gave to nos. 59 and 61 in the *Convivio*. These are followed by the two definitely doctrinal canzoni, nos. 69 and 70 (with no. 71 as a pendant to them) which in Barbi are interspersed with the preceding series of love-poems; and these in turn by Dante's first venture into the low or 'comic' style, the sonnet-exchange with Forese Donati (placed earlier by Barbi to form his Book III, nos. LXXIII–LXXVIII). As in Barbi's ordering, the pre-exilic poems are completed by the 'rime petrose', nos. 77–80.

It must be emphasized that these alterations are made without any pretension to fix definitively the *real* chronology of the poems concerned (a thing in any case almost certainly impossible). Their general purpose is to mark out clearly, while respecting what is *known* of the 'real' chronology, the stages of Dante's poetic development;

and it is certain that in the period between the *Vita Nuova* and the exile, doctrinal verse, the 'low' style, and the 'stile aspro' of nos. 77–80, were innovations with respect to Dante's earlier procedures.

The other alteration that should be mentioned is our regrouping of the sonnet-correspondence between Dante and Cino da Pistoia. This was divided by Barbi into two groups: pre-exilic (nos. XCIV–XCVII) and post-exilic (CX–CXV). Chronologically there is much to be said for this division, but for our purpose it seemed more convenient, in this one case, to ignore the claims of strict chronology and place all these sonnets together after no. CVI (here no. 83) which was certainly written in exile. For further discussion of this point, see the introductory note below to nos. 84*a*–88*a*; and for arguments justifying the other alterations mentioned above, see especially the introductory notes to nos. 8–24, 25, 72–74.

As is clear, we have used Arabic numerals for all the poems in this volume; Barbi's Roman numerals being added, in brackets, at the head of each poem. Every poem not written by Dante is distinguished by a letter placed after the number indicating the poem by Dante to which it is a reply (or, as in no. 57*a*, on which it is a comment) or which is a reply to it: thus 15*a* is Cavalcanti's reply to no. 15; and Cino's sonnet, replied to by Dante's no. 84, is 84*a*. Only in one case are more than two poems involved; Dante's sonnet indicated by no. 6 provoked three replies, and these are numbered 6*a*, 6*b*, 6*c*.

Something must be said in general on the commentaries on the poems, in the second volume. The purpose of these is both to elucidate meaning and to call attention to significant features of Dante's style. The elucidation of meaning has naturally entailed much discussion of words and usage, and abundant reference to Dante's other works, to earlier and contemporary Italian authors, and,

xl

to a lesser extent, to poets in Provençal. This work of reference has been much facilitated by the very ample anthology of thirteenth-century Italian poetry, superbly edited by Contini, *Poeti del Duecento*, Milan–Naples, 2 vols., 1960. For the sake of brevity this anthology is often cited with a simple page and line reference. Where the interpretation of a poem required biographical information, we have tried to supply this (in the special case of no. 59 the biographical discussion involved outran the limits of a mere note, and so had to be deferred to an Appendix at the end of the volume). Since the poems are accompanied by prose translations, it has been possible to limit the interpretative discussions in the commentary to such terms and usages as may be expected to present difficulties to readers who are not familiar with early Italian. On the other hand our desire to make the notes on each poem fairly complete in themselves has led us (while giving abundant cross-references) to repeat the glosses on certain words (e.g. *però*), where otherwise it would not be easy to avoid confusion.

The elucidation of a poet's meaning may lead inevitably to discussing his manner of treating a subject, for example where one has to ask whether or no he is using allegory. But our discussion of the stylistic features of Dante's *Rime* has been taken far beyond the limits that the determination of levels of meaning would require. This is because, though we have been sparing with value-judgements on the poems, we have emphatically considered them as poems—as works of art ; moreover as works belonging to a very definite literary and cultural context. The technical rhetorical terms used in the commentary, and a good deal of the stylistic analysis, presuppose in the reader at least some knowledge of the literary tradition the various aspects of which have been explored by such scholars as L. Arbusow,

E. Auerbach, C. Baldwin, E. R. Curtius, F. Di Capua, E. Faral, C. H. Haskins, A. Marigo, A. Schiaffini (see the Bibliography, vol. 2, pp. 363–71). Aware, on the other hand, of the danger of missing the wood for the trees, we have given particular attention to the overall *structure* of the poems, and especially of the canzoni. We cannot assume that every reader will be interested in every point we have discussed; we have only tried to ensure, firstly, that no important problem of interpretation or point of style has been passed over, and secondly, that the material is presented in such a way as should permit—with the help of the Index Rerum at the end of the volume—fairly easy consultation on any point in particular.

Our enormous debt to previous workers in this field will be obvious to every reader. Mention has been made of some of the more outstanding scholars whose labours during the past half-century have thrown so much light on the technical aspects of medieval literature. Even more apparent will be our debt to those—and they are mostly Italians—who have worked on Dante's *Rime* in particular. Our debt to Michele Barbi is, of course, simply that of all modern students of the *Rime*; he laid the foundations on which we all must build. The influence of Contini's brilliant commentary (Turin, 2nd edition, 1946) is impressed on almost every page of the present work. On the early Italian lyric in general Contini is the unrivalled master; and as regards Dante's *Rime* in particular, he is the critic who has most clearly shown how consummate scholarship can deepen and sharpen a sense of their quality as poetry. To his example, his taste, and his intelligence we owe more than we can say. Most useful also has been the ample and notably independent commentary of Daniele Mattalia (*D. A. Le Rime*, Turin, 1943), particularly in respect of the doctrinal and moral canzoni; and, for Dante's earlier poetry, the work of Francesco Maggini, resuming and supplementing that of Barbi (*Rime della 'Vita Nuova' e della giovinezza*, vol. ii of the 'Edizione Nazionale', Florence, 1956). We owe much too to Domenico De Robertis, particularly for his penetrating study of the *Vita Nuova* (*Il libro della 'V.N.'*, Florence, 1960) and for his fundamental researches into the manuscript tradition of the earlier *Rime* (see especially *Il canzoniere Escorialense e la tradizione 'veneziana' delle rime dello stil novo*, Turin, 1954).

The first merit which we feel entitled to claim for our own work is that it represents the first attempt on a large scale to introduce English readers to the results, synthesized and critically assessed, of recent Italian scholarship in this sector of Dante studies. We would also, however, venture to claim that our treatment of many problems, both interpretative and stylistic, that are posed by the *Rime* is on the whole more thorough than that provided by any single commentary hitherto published.

A word may be added on the respective contributions to the work as a whole of Dr. Boyde and myself. Our collaboration has been very close—and enjoyable—over the whole field and at every point. But Dr. Boyde's special competence in the field of medieval rhetoric and verse-style means that he is chiefly responsible for the stylistic material in the notes. To him also is mainly due the re-ordering of the sequence of the *Rime* described above. I have had the larger share in preparing the biographical material, and in the interpretation of Dante's thought in the light of medieval philosophy and—on the few occasions where this is directly relevant—theology.

KENELM FOSTER

NOTE ON DANTE'S METRIC
AND VERSIFICATION

Dante's Metric

THE following sketch outlines the principles governing the structure of the metrical forms used by Dante, and introduces the necessary technical terms and conventional symbols used in the analyses of Dante's metric given in the commentary. The description is limited to Dante's practice and theory, and although much of it has wider validity it should not be simply taken for granted that any particular feature is true either of earlier or of later poets. It does not attempt to cover all the topics mentioned by Dante in this connexion: the interested reader should consult the *De vulgari eloquentia* itself (ii. viii–xiv, ed. A. Marigo, 3rd ed., Florence, 1957).

Dante was not an innovator in his metric, and with a few notable exceptions he confined himself to the three metrical forms which had come to predominate in the earlier Italian poets: the canzone, the ballata, and the sonnet. The principles governing them all are to be found in the canzone (cf. *DVE* ii. iii, viii. 6–7), and accordingly it is this, the most illustrious form, that will be described first.

Canzone

As its name suggests, the canzone was originally a lyric in the strict sense of the word. In Provence, where the genre had originated nearly 200 years before Dante first attempted it in the mid 1280s, it had been normal for the poet to write the words, compose the melody, and even perform his own *cansos* (although in course of time specialization inevitably set in). In the Italian tradition however, where the earliest surviving canzoni date from *c.* 1230, the poet did not compose the melody for his lyric, and ordinarily the canzone was not set to music at all—this being a fact which had important consequences for the development of the genre in Italy. Nevertheless, although the Italian canzone was not set, it still had to be 'settable': *omnis stantia ad quandam odam recipiendam armonizata est* (*DVE* II. x. 2). Thus, although it was a 'literary' and not a 'lyric' poem, its form was still determined by musical conventions.

A canzone usually consisted of from five to seven stanzas, each necessarily of identical design since the same melody or sequence of melodies was repeated for each stanza. It could, however, be complete in one stanza, as in nos. 9, 22, and 46 in this volume. A stanza might be set to one continuous melody (as in the special case of no. 78 below), but in the vast majority of cases it would be set to two contrasted melodies, at least one of which had to be repeated within the stanza. So, according to Dante, the possible sequence of melodies, and thus of the constituent parts of the stanza, were I; I+I+II; I+II+II; I+I+II+II. Dante indeed admitted (*DVE* II. x. 4; xi. 10) that a melody might be repeated more than once within the stanza, but he himself never wrote a canzone of that type. Note that these musical conventions made it impossible for a stanza to be constructed simply of two indivisible parts, I+II, and that far and away the most common type in the Italian tradition is I+I+II.

The part of the stanza to be set to the first melody is called by Dante the *frons*: where the first melody is to be repeated, the two equal parts are called *pedes*. The part to be set to the second melody is called by Dante the *sirima* (*sirma*) or *cauda*; where this melody is to be repeated the equal parts are called by him *versus*: however, in order not to confuse the reader, we have preferred (in its Latin form) the term which has prevailed in Italian, *voltae*. Note, too, that we depart from Dante's usage by occasionally referring to the whole of the first or second parts as the *frons* or *sirima*, even when these are composed of *pedes* and *voltae*.

The rhythmic structure of any *pes*, *frons*, *volta*, or *sirima* was severely limited by the fact that, in the Italian tradition, they were almost invariably constructed of lines of verse containing either eleven or seven syllables. Only in one canzone (no. 70) does Dante include the penta-syllable, and even there he does not use more than two per stanza, one in each *pes*, as his theory demanded (*DVE* II. xii. 7). Nevertheless, by varying the number of lines (e.g. Dante's *pedes* have from three to six lines, his *sirimas* from five to twelve), by varying the *relative* lengths of *frons* and *sirima*, and above all by weaving together hendecasyllables and heptasyllables in differing proportions and sequences, the poet could and did do a great deal to differentiate one canzone from another—as a glance at the twenty-one regular canzoni in this book will show.

The variety obtained by these purely rhythmic means obviously seemed less important to the poets than that which they could achieve by repeating the sounds which terminated each line (*desinentie carminum*, *DVE* II. xiii. 4) in differing sequences, in order to create different patterns of rhyme. Rhyme[1] was the distinguishing feature of Romance vernacular verse; by extension, poems could be called simply 'rhymes';[2] and it was to the elaboration of rhyme-schemes (*relatio rithimorum*) that poets devoted their greatest efforts: '. . . *sciendum est quod in hoc amplis-simam sibi licentiam fere omnes assumunt; et ex hoc maxime*

---

[1] '. . . strettamente [rima] s'intende pur per quella concordanza che ne l'ultima e penultima sillaba far si suole . . .' *Con.* IV. ii. 12.

[2] '. . . largamente . . . [rima] s'intende per tutto quel parlare che 'n numeri e tempo regolato in rimate consonanze cade . . .', ibid.

totius armonie dulcedo intenditur' (*DVE* II. xiii. 3). It should be noted that by Dante's time it was customary, although still not obligatory (*DVE* II. xiii. 4–5), for every line to be 'bound' by rhyme to at least one other within the stanza. By then, too, it would have been exceptional for successive stanzas to share not just the same rhyme-scheme but the same rhyme-*sounds* (although this type—in Provençal terminology *coblas unissonans* as opposed to *coblas singulars*—was the most common among the troubadours, and had been cultivated by the Sicilians). Similarly, it would have been exceptional for a line to be rhymed not within the stanza but with the corresponding line in successive stanzas (*vers dissolut*: see the introductory note to no. 78 for a fuller discussion). Except in no. 25, Dante himself allows only the first line of a *congedo* to stand unrhymed (cf. notes on the ballata, p. xlix below). In the commentary these unrhymed lines have been indicated with the letter X. This is a convenient point to call attention to two other conventions used in the metrical analysis. Where a stanza is built up with two different types of line, the shorter is represented by a small instead of a capital letter: thus the rhyme-scheme of the opening lines of the first canzone in this book (no. 9) is represented: a B b C. The division between *frons* and *sirima* is shown by a colon, and that between *pedes* or *voltae* by a semi-colon.

Among the conventions which limited the possible distribution of the rhymes, we may note the following.

(*a*) Dante insists (*DVE* II. xiii. 8–9) that every line in the *pedes* must be rhymed with at least one other in the *pedes*. And in practice Dante is a little more rigid than in his theory, for in the second *pes* he always repeats all the terminations of the first, whether or not these had already been rhymed within that *pes*. Thus he uses schemes like ABBA; ABBA (no. 46): ABBC; ABBC (no. 61): ABC; ABC (no. 13): but not ABB; ACC, although this is permissible in theory, and he will use such a pattern in *voltae* (e.g. no. 33). It was not necessary to repeat the terminations in the same order as they had appeared in the first *pes*, e.g. one might prefer ABC; BAC (no. 59), or ABbA; BAaB (no. 22): but if one took this liberty of 'inverting the rhymes' one would have to do so in every stanza.

(*b*) By Dante's time the *frons* and *sirima* were usually contrasted not only rhythmically but in their rhyme-sounds. But Dante notes one important exception to this convention (*DVE* II. xiii. 6): it was common practice to rhyme the first line of the *sirima* with the last line of the *frons*, and this one rhyme-sound from the *frons* could then be used again in the *sirima* (e.g. nos. 9, 22, 33, etc.). When the two parts of the stanza are thus linked—and Dante only once fails to make this *concatenatio pulcra*—the first line of the *sirima* is known in Italian as the 'key line', *verso chiave* (used in this way the term is not Dante's).

(*c*) Dante liked to mark the close of a stanza by rhyming the last two lines together (*combinatio desinentiarum ultimarum*, *DVE* II. xiii. 10) because *pulcerrime . . . se habent ultimorum carminum desinentie si cum rithimo in silentium cadant* (ibid. 7). In the metrical analyses in the commentary, the *verso chiave* and the final couplet have been marked off by commas.

(*d*) Dante only once uses internal rhyme (*rimalmezzo*), which was very common in his predecessors (in no. 70, but probably also in the isolated stanza no. 9: see the notes to those poems for further discussion).

Here is one stanza—typical of Dante's love-canzoni—to illustrate many of the features described above. Note in particular how the syntax is determined by the metrical form. Scheme: AbC; AcB: B, DEeD, FF.

Pes 1   E' si raccoglie ne li miei sospiri
           un sono di pietate,
           che va chiamando Morte tuttavia:

Pes 2   a lei si volser tutti i miei disiri,
(with inversion   quando la donna mia
  of rhymes)   fu giunta da la sua crudelitate;

verso chiave   perché 'l piacere de la sua bieltate
                         partendo sé da la nostra veduta,
                         divenne spirital bellezza grande,
Sirima.   che per lo cielo spande
                         luce d'amor, che li angeli saluta,
    final couplet { e lo intelletto loro alto, sottile
                       { face maravigliar, sì v'è gentile.

                                        (no. 49. 14–26)

A full-length canzone was traditionally rounded off by a kind of postscript or valediction in which the poet addressed himself to his poem and 'took his leave of it' (whence the normal Italian terms *congedo*, *commiato*: Dante himself uses the word *tornata*, *Con.* II. xi). The remarkably varied and original use to which Dante put this traditional feature is illustrated in the commentaries. Metrically it is sufficient to note that the *congedo* may be identical with the preceding stanzas (as in nos. 33, 61), or it may have the scheme of the *sirimas* of the preceding stanzas (e.g. nos. 32, 77, 80), or it may be quite independent (e.g. nos. 13, 25, 47, etc.). Three of the full-length canzoni however have no *congedo* (nos. 40, 67, 70).

Ballata

In most respects the ballata may be regarded as a simpler form of the canzone. Thus it may consist of several identical stanzas (no. 24) or it may be complete in one (no. 23). It is *invariably* formed of two *pedes* and an indivisible *sirima* (the nomenclature is, strictly, distinct, these parts being called the *mutationes* and *volta* respectively). The *pedes*, which do not normally have more than three lines, are subject to the same rhyming conventions as those in the canzone. The *sirima* almost always opens with a *verso chiave* and does not usually have more than four lines (where these numbers are exceeded there is usually a majority of heptasyllables: so, for example, in Cavalcanti's *Fresca rosa novella* and *Perch' i' no spero*). The distinguishing feature is that the ballata *always* opens with a *ripresa* (*responsorium* in *DVE* II. viii. 8), stating the theme of the whole poem, this *ripresa* being metrically identical with the *sirima* of the following stanza or stanzas. If the ballata was set to music the *ripresa* would be repeated after every stanza—whence its name: the sequence of melodies would thus be: II (*ripresa*), I–I (*pedes*), II (*sirima*), II (*ripresa*), etc. (Note, however, that in contrast to the *riprese* in a Poliziano or a Lorenzo de' Medici, those in the ballatas of Dante and his circle were not usually refrain-like in character.) The last line of the *ripresa* is *invariably* rhymed with the last line in all the *sirimas*, which may thus be unrhymed within the stanza. Thus the scheme of no. 23 is: *Ripresa* YZZY. *Stanza* ABc; BAc: C,DDY.

Of the various species of ballata (these being distinguished only by the size of the stanza), we need consider only two. The *ballata grande* (e.g. nos. 23, 24, 60) has a *ripresa/sirima* of four lines, of which at least three must be hendecasyllables; whilst the *pedes* have at least two hendecasyllables (no. 60), and usually a third line (nos. 23, 24). The *ballata mezzana* (nos. 21, 65, 66) has only three lines in the *ripresa/sirima*, and the *pedes* normally have only two lines (possibly three, if at least two are heptasyllables).

Sonnet

The 'regular' Italian or Petrarchan sonnet—unlike the English or Shakespearean variety—may be treated as a standardized canzone stanza. It *invariably* has two *pedes* of four hendecasyllables each, and two *voltae* of three.

1

Only two rhymes are allowed in the *pedes*, and they must be disposed according to one of the following schemes: ABAB; ABAB (*rima alternata*, the more archaic pattern): or ABBA; ABBA (*rima incrociata*). The *voltae* may have either two or three rhymes, all distinct from those in the *pedes* (i.e. there is never a *verso chiave*). Dante subjects the *voltae* of his sonnets to the same restrictions as those noted in the *pedes* of his canzoni. Thus, although he varies the order in which he repeats the terminations of the first *volta*, he always repeats them all and never introduces a new sound in the second *volta*: CDC; CDC: or CDC; DCD: or CDD; DCC: or CDE; CDE: or CDE; EDC: or CDE; DCE: but *not* CDD; CEE as in the *voltae* of a canzone, e.g. no. 33.

The form of the 'double' sonnet—used three times by Dante—is described in the notes to no. 8. There are further discussions of points of metric in the introductory notes to nos. 9, 21, 25, 33, 45, 46, 70, 78, 79.

VERSIFICATION

Italian versification is both syllabic and dynamic: in other words, for a line or verse to be such it must have the requisite number of syllables (due allowance having been made for elision and coalescence of contiguous vowels, and for exceptional hiatus and diaereses),[1] and the words that form the line must be so arranged that their stressed syllables fall in certain positions.

[1] Hiatus (*dialefe* = absence of elision, *sinalefe*) is *normal* when either the final vowel of the first word or the initial vowel of the following word carries a linguistic stress: *così* ‖ *àlta* is thus doubly normal. Diaeresis (*dierisi* = absence of coalescence, *sinerisi*) is *normal* in words where the second of two contiguous vowels carries the stress, and the first vowel is an *a*, *e*, or *o*, e.g. in words like *pàura*, *bĕáto*, *sŏáve*, and also when the contiguous vowels occur in rhyme (see some of the examples on p. liii). In the early poets, 'exceptional' hiatus and diaereses are in fact not uncommon: the latter have been indicated in the text, e.g. no. 25. 5 *avēan*; no. 32. 61, *passíon*.

All lines have a stressed syllable in the penultimate position, the position of the other stresses varying with the type of line. For lines with an even number of syllables (never used by Dante, cf. *DVE* II. v. 7) the accentual patterns are regulated rigidly, as they are also in the nine-syllable line used in no. 21 (cf. *DVE* II. v. 6); but they are remarkably flexible in the two lines usually employed by Dante, the heptasyllable and the hendecasyllable, particularly in the latter, *quorum omnium . . . videtur esse superbius, tam temporis occupatione, quam capacitate sententie, constructionis et vocabulorum* (*DVE* II. v. 3).

Apart from its invariable stress in the tenth position, a normal hendecasyllable will have a stressed syllable in either the fourth or sixth positions, e.g.:

4–10	*con una vóce*	*che sovente ména*
4–10	*partendo sé*	*da la nostra vedúta*
6–10	*del viso d'una dònna*	*che vi míra*
6–10	*convenemi parlár*	*traendo guái*

As in these examples, there is usually a caesura—of greatly varying 'strength'—immediately after the word bearing this the dominant stress in the line, the line being thus articulated into two unequal hemistiches. Those lines which begin with the shorter hemistich (with the dominant stress in the fourth position, hence caesura falling either after the fourth or, usually, the fifth position) are termed *a minore*: those which begin with the longer hemistich (caesura falling after sixth or seventh positions) are termed *a maiore*.

In nearly all cases there is at least one other stressed syllable in the longer hemistich, which usually falls in the second or third positions in the *a maiore* species, and in the seventh or eighth positions in the *a minore*. A line may however contain anything from two to five stressed syllables and Dante makes use of an amazing number of accentual schemes—far more than came to be accepted by Petrarch and later poets. Note however that stresses in the ninth position are not common and those in the fifth very rare indeed, as both would tend to 'interfere' with the all important dominant and fixed stresses. It will perhaps be helpful to give examples of the fifteen accentual patterns most common in Dante's lyrics to demonstrate the variety of movement *normal* in his hendecasyllables, and, incidentally, to illustrate the rules of scansion.

They are quoted in descending order of frequency in his use.[1]

2–4–8–10	*Ne li occhi porta la mia donna Amore*
2–6–10	*Fu posta da l'altissimo signore*
4–8–10	*La qualità de la mia vita oscura*
2–6–8–10	*Un spirito soave pien d'amore*
4–7–10	*E se venite da tanta pietate*
2–4–7–10	*Mi pose in vita sì dolce e soave*
1–4–8–10	*Dànnomi angoscia li sospiri forte*
1–4–7–10	*Escono spirti d'amore inflammati*
2–4–6–8–10	*Ancor che ciel con ciel in punto sià*
2–4–6–8–10	*Bieltate appare in saggia donna pui*
3–6–10	*Maraviglia ne l'atto che procede*
3–6–8–10	*Che m'infiammano il cor ch'io porto anciso*
2–6–7–10	*E tanto è la stagion forte ed acerba*

---

[1] These assertions are based on the analysis of all the poems included by Dante in the *Vita Nuova*, that is 31 out of the first 57 in this volume and a representative selection of later poems, viz. nos. 59–61, 69, 70, 77, 80, 81, 83, 84–88. About two-thirds of the 1,300 hendecasyllables analysed conform to one of these fifteen schemes.

4–6–10   *Che si movéan le lágrime dal córe*

2–4–6–10   *Quantúnque vólte lásso mi rimémbra*

In Dante's hendecasyllables, two of the stressed syllables, and thus the rhythmic pulses, fall in even-number positions (10, 4, or 6); two of the odd-number positions (5, 9) are usually avoided; the 'optional' pulses are more common in even-number positions than in odd; to this extent the line is more iambic in character than trochaic, dactylic, or anapaestic. On the other hand, pulses in the first, third, and seventh positions occur frequently even in these most common schemes, as do sequences of two or three unstressed syllables; only about 20 per cent. of Dante's hendecasyllables have five stressed syllables; and in the 33 per cent. that do not share one of the schemes exemplified above, Dante often allows stressed syllables to fall in adjacent positions. There are, in addition, a number of verses which do not belong to either the *a minore* or the *a maiore* family; and for all these reasons it is comparatively rare in a poem by Dante for an iambic pattern to impose itself on the ear.

RHYME

In Italian, as in English, two words can rhyme when they are identical in sound from and including the vowel of the stressed syllable to the end of the word. Note however that, as most Italian words are paroxytones, almost all Italian rhymes are 'feminine' by English standards: *amore-core*. If one is to be fully alert to the ways in which rhyme was handled by Dante and his contemporaries, one should be aware of the following species:

(*a*) *Rima ricca*. The consonant which *opens* the stressed syllable is often common to both rhyme-words: e.g. no. 26—varie*tate*, potes*tate*, pie*tate*; no. 28—*more*, A*more*, tre*more*; no. 34—ra*gione*, ma*gione*, sta*gione*.

(*b*) *Rima derivativa.* In some cases of *rima ricca*, one of the words is actually 'formed' from the other by the addition of a prefix: e.g. no. 84*a*—*dice-disdice, perde-disperde.*

(*c*) *Rima equivoca.* The words in rhyme may be homophones, but distinct in sense: e.g. no. 89. 36, 37—*sole* ('is accustomed', 'sun'); no. 47. 50, 53—*parte* ('part', 'separates'); no. 68. 99, 102—*prove* (2nd pers. pres. subj., 3rd pers.).

(*d*) *Rima 'identica'* (*du même au même*). Very occasionally the words are in fact perfectly identical. There is no true example in Dante's *Rime*, but see note to no. 74.11, and introductory note to no. 78.

(*e*) *Rima composta.* Two or more words may be put together to make the rhyme; e.g. no. 40. 41–42—*crucciati, morra'ti*; ibid. 59, 62 *cielo, dire'lo*. See in particular the notes to nos. 3*a* and 4.

(*f*) *Rima tronca.* It is possible for the rhyme-words to be oxytones, that is, stressed on the final syllable, e.g. *Inf.* IV. 56, *Noè, re, fé*; *Inf.* XXXII. 62, *Artù, più, fu*. Note that (*a*) unlike in English these oxytones must end in a vowel; (*b*) they are very rare and certainly excluded from the 'high' style (in this book only in no. 21); (*c*) the stressed syllable still falls in the penultimate position in the line— in other words, the line lacks the final unstressed syllable but has an otherwise normal accentual scheme.

(*g*) *Rima sdrucciola.* It is also possible for the rhyme-words to be proparoxytones, that is, stressed on the antepenultimate syllable, e.g. *Inf.* XV. 1 *margini, argini*. Again this form was rare in Dante's time (only in no. 70. 33–34 here), and again the stressed syllable falls in the penultimate position, the verse merely having an additional unstressed syllable at the end.　　PATRICK BOYDE

THE POEMS

Ia (B. XXXIX)

DANTE DA MAIANO A DIVERSI RIMATORI

Provedi, saggio, ad esta visïone,
e per mercé ne trai vera sentenza.
Dico: una donna di bella fazone,
di cu' el meo cor gradir molto s'agenza,

mi fé d'una ghirlanda donagione,   5
verde, fronzuta, con bella accoglienza:
appresso mi trovai per vestigione
camicia di suo dosso, a mia parvenza.

Allor di tanto, amico, mi francai,
che dolcemente presila abbracciare: 10
non si contese, ma ridea la bella.

Così ridendo, molto la baciai:
del più non dico, ché mi fé giurare.
E morta, ch'è mia madre, era con ella.

I (B. XL)

RISPOSTA DI DANTE ALIGHIERI

Savete giudicar vostra ragione,
o om che pregio di saver portate;
per che, vitando aver con voi quistione.
com so rispondo a le parole ornate.

Disio verace, u' rado fin si pone,   5
che mosse di valore o di bieltate,
imagina l'amica oppinïone
significasse il don che pria narrate.

I*a*

You who are intelligent, consider this vision and please show its true meaning. It was like this: a fair woman, in gaining whose favour my heart takes much pleasure, made me a gift of a green leafy garland; and charmingly she did so. And then I seemed to find myself clothed in a shift that she had worn.

Then I made so bold as gently to embrace her. The fair one did not resist, but smiled; and as she smiled I kissed her repeatedly. I will not say what followed—she made me swear not to. And a dead woman—my mother—was with her.

I

DANTE ALIGHIERI'S REPLY

You know how to interpret your theme, intelligent as you are; so I will not enter into any dispute with you, but only answer as best I can your elegantly phrased question. My view—speaking as a friend—is that the gift you first mention signified true desire, proceeding from merit or beauty, a desire that seldom comes to an end.

Lo vestimento, aggiate vera spene
che fia, da lei cui desïate, amore;
e 'n ciò provide vostro spirto bene:

dico, pensando l'ovra sua d'allore.
La figura che già morta sorvene
è la fermezza ch'averà nel core.

2 (B. XLI)

DANTE ALIGHIERI A DANTE DA MAIANO[1]

Per pruova di saper com vale o quanto
lo mastro l'oro, adducelo a lo foco;
e, ciò faccendo, chiara e sa se poco,
amico, di pecunia vale o tanto.

Ed eo, per levar prova del meo canto,   5
l'adduco a voi, cui paragone voco
di ciascun c'have in canoscenza loco,
o che di pregio porti loda o vanto.

E chero a voi col meo canto più saggio
che mi deggiate il dol maggio d'Amore   10
qual'è, per vostra scienza, nominare:

e ciò non movo per quistioneggiare
(ché già inver voi so non avria valore),
ma per saver ciò ch'eo vaglio e varraggio.

2a (B. XLII)

DANTE DA MAIANO A DANTE ALIGHIERI

Qual che voi siate, amico, vostro manto
di scienza parmi tal, che non è gioco;
sì che, per non saver, d'ira mi coco,
non che laudarvi, sodisfarvi tanto.

[1] See above, p. xxxviii.

4

As for the garment, be confident that this will be love, given by her whom you desire, as indeed your spirit well divined—I say this in view of the act that followed. The dead figure that came on the scene is the constancy that she'll now bear in her heart.

2

The goldsmith, to test the value of gold, brings it to the fire; and so doing, establishes whether it is worth little or much. And I, to test my poem, bring it to you whom I call the Paragon of all who are numbered among the intelligent, or are praised or honoured for merit.

And so, writing with all the skill I can command, I ask you to tell me, from your knowledge of the subject, what is the greatest suffering caused by love. Not that I wish to join with you in argument—knowing that I should be no match for you—but I want to know what I am worth now and what I shall be worth.

2a

Whoever you may be, my friend, it seems that you are arrayed in such learning as commands respect; so that I burn with rage at not being able even to satisfy your

Sacciate ben (ch'io mi conosco alquanto)   5
che di saver ver voi ho men d'un moco,
né per via saggia come voi non voco,
così parete saggio in ciascun canto.

Poi piacevi saver lo meo coraggio,
e io 'l vi mostro di menzogna fore,   10
sì come quei ch'a saggio è 'l suo parlare:

certanamente a mia coscienza pare,
chi non è amato, s'elli è amadore,
che 'n cor porti dolor senza paraggio.

3 (B. XLIII)

DANTE ALIGHIERI A DANTE DA MAIANO

Lo vostro fermo dir fino ed orrato
approva ben ciò bon ch'om di voi parla,
ed ancor più, ch'ogni uom fora gravato
di vostra loda intera nominarla;

ché il vostro pregio in tal loco è poggiato,   5
che propiamente om nol poria contarla:
però qual vera loda al vostro stato
crede parlando dar, dico disparla.

Dite ch'amare e non essere amato
ène lo dol che più d'Amore dole,   10
e manti dicon che più v'ha dol maggio:

onde umil prego non vi sia disgrato
vostro saver che chiari ancor, se vole,
se 'l vero, o no, di ciò mi mostra saggio.

6

curiosity, let alone praise you as you deserve. Know that my knowledge (for I do know myself a little) is less than a pea compared with yours; nor do I row my boat on a wise course as you do, so wise do you show yourself in every way.

Since, then, it pleases you to know my heart, I'll show it to you sincerely, as addressing a man of intelligence. It seems clear to me that the lover who is not loved has in his heart the greatest pain of all.

3

DANTE ALIGHIERI TO DANTE DA MAIANO

Your assured, elegant, dignified speech bears good witness to the good that men say of you: indeed it does more, so that everyone would be hard put to it to recite your praises completely—no words would be adequate to recount them, your merit has soared so high. Hence I say that whoever thinks he justly praises you in fact speaks ill of you.

You say that to love unloved is the worst of love's pains. Yet many say there is a still greater pain. So I beg you, if you don't mind, in your wisdom, please, to throw yet more light on the matter, showing me whether or no experience declares the truth of it.

3a (B. XLIV)

DANTE DA MAIANO A DANTE ALIGHIERI

Non canoscendo, amico, vostro nomo,
donde che mova chi con meco parla,
conosco ben che scienz'à di gran nomo,
sì che di quanti saccio nessun par l'à:

ché si pò ben canoscere d'un omo,   5
ragionando, se ha senno, che ben par là;
conven poi voi laudar sanza far nomo,
è forte a lingua mia di ciò com parla.

Amico (certo sonde, acciò ch'amato
per amore aggio), sacci ben, chi ama,   10
se non è amato, lo maggior dol porta;

ché tal dolor ten sotto suo camato
tutti altri, e capo di ciascun si chiama:
da ciò ven quanta pena Amore porta.

4 (B. XLV)

DANTE ALIGHIERI A DANTE DA MAIANO

Lasso, lo dol che più mi dole e serra
è ringraziar, ben non sapendo como;
per me più saggio converriasi, como
vostro saver, ched ogni quistion serra.

Del dol, che manta gente dite serra,   5
è tal voler qual voi lor non ha como;
e 'l proprio sì disio saver dol, como
di ciò sovente, dico, essendo a serra.

3a

DANTE DA MAIANO TO DANTE ALIGHIERI

Although I don't know your name or birthplace—you, my friend, who write to me—yet I know well that he has famous knowledge, such that no one I know has so much. For one can easily recognize from his conversation whether a man is intelligent—that's where it shows! Since I have to praise you without naming you, my tongue is in difficulties, as it speaks of this.

Know, my friend (and I am certain of this, as one who has loved with real love) that he who loves unloved has the greatest pain; for this pain holds sway over all others and is called the chief one: it is the source of all the suffering that love brings.

4

DANTE ALIGHIERI TO DANTE DA MAIANO

Alas, what most pains and grips me is the pain of thanking you, not knowing how: there should be a wiser man in my place, one with wisdom like yours that clinches every argument. As for the pain which, you say, grips many people, it is a longing which affects you differently from them. But I desire to understand this suffering precisely, being, as I say, one who is often gripped by it.

Però pregh'eo ch'argomentiate, saggio,
d'autorità mostrando ciò che porta
di voi la 'mpresa, acciò che sia più chiara;

e poi parrà, parlando di ciò, chiara,
quale più chiarirem dol pena porta,
d'ello assegnando, amico, prov'e saggio.

5a (B. XLVI)

DANTE DA MAIANO A DANTE ALIGHIERI

Amor mi fa sì fedelmente amare
e sì distretto m'have en suo disire,
che solo un'ora non poria partire
lo core mëo da lo suo pensare.

D'Ovidio ciò mi son miso a provare
che disse per lo mal d'Amor guarire,
e ciò ver me non val mai che mentire;
per ch'eo mi rendo a sol merzé chiamare.

E ben conosco omai veracemente
che 'nverso Amor non val forza ned arte,
ingegno né leggenda ch'omo trovi,

mai che merzede ed esser sofferente
e ben servir: così n'have omo parte.
Provedi, amico saggio, se l'approvi.

5 (B. XLVII)

RISPOSTA DI DANTE ALIGHIERI

Savere e cortesia, ingegno ed arte,
nobilitate, bellezza e riccore,
fortezza e umiltate e largo core,
prodezza ed eccellenza, giunte e sparte,

Therefore, I beg you, wise as you are, to show reasons drawn from authorities to prove what your thesis contains, so that it shine out with more lustre. This clarification effected through discussion, we shall then establish which suffering brings the most pain, proving our conclusion, friend, by reason and experience.

5a

Love makes me love so constantly and he has so bound me in his will that not even for one hour could my heart leave thinking of him. I have set myself to test what Ovid prescribed as remedy for lovesickness; but so far as I'm concerned it is simply a lie: hence I resign myself to begging for pity.

And now I know it for a fact that neither strength nor skill avails against Love, neither natural wit nor any available teaching: nothing but pity and patience and loyal service; such is the way to have dealings with him. Give this, my intelligent friend, your attention and tell me whether you agree.

5

DANTE ALIGHIERI'S REPLY

Knowledge and courtesy; natural wit and acquired skill; nobility, beauty, wealth; strength and gentleness and generosity; valour and high distinction—these gifts and virtues, combined or separate, in all cases win love

este grazie e vertuti in onne parte 5
con lo piacer di lor vincono Amore:
una più ch'altra ben ha più valore
inverso lui, ma ciascuna n'ha parte.

Onde se voli, amico, che ti vaglia
vertute naturale od accidente, 10
con lealtà in piacer d'Amor l'adovra,

e non a contastar sua graziosa ovra:
ché nulla cosa gli è incontro possente,
volendo prender om con lui battaglia.

6 (B.1)

DANTE AI FEDELI D'AMORE

A ciascun'alma presa e gentil core
nel cui cospetto ven lo dir presente,
in ciò che mi rescrivan suo parvente,
salute in lor segnor, cioè Amore.

Già eran quasi che atterzate l'ore 5
del tempo che onne stella n'è lucente,
quando m'apparve Amor subitamente,
cui essenza membrar mi dà orrore.

Allegro mi sembrava Amor tenendo
meo core in mano, e ne le braccia avea 10
madonna involta in un drappo dormendo.

Poi la svegliava, e d'esto core ardendo
lei paventosa umilmente pascea:
appresso gir lo ne vedea piangendo.

over with their attraction: one may have more power with him than another, but each has a share in it.

Therefore, my friend, if you want natural virtue or any added quality to be of use to you, set them to work faithfully to do Love's will, and not to oppose his gracious working. For nothing avails against Love, supposing one chooses to fight him.

6

DANTE ALIGHIERI TO OTHER POETS

To every captive soul and gentle heart into whose sight this poem may come, that each may write back to me what he makes of it, a greeting in his lord, that is Love. Already almost a third of the hours had passed by of the time in which all the stars shine clear, when suddenly Love appeared to me in a form that is terrifying to remember.

Love seemed joyful, holding my heart in his hand, while in his arms he had my lady wrapped in a cloth, asleep. Then he awoke her and, though she was afraid, he humbly fed her with this heart which was burning. Then I saw him go away weeping.

6a (B. II)

RISPOSTA DI GUIDO CAVALCANTI

Vedeste, al mio parere, onne valore
e tutto gioco e quanto bene om sente,
se foste in prova del segnor valente
che segnoreggia il mondo de l'onore,

poi vive in parte dove noia more   5
e tien ragion nel cassar de la mente;
sì va soave per sonni a la gente,
che 'l cor ne porta senza far dolore.

Di voi lo core ne portò, veggendo
che vostra donna alla morte cadea: 10
nodrilla dello cor, di ciò temendo.

Quando v'apparve che sen gia dogliendo,
fu 'l dolce sonno ch'allor si compiea,
ché 'l su' contraro lo venia vincendo.

6b (B. III)

RISPOSTA DI CINO DA PISTOIA (O TERINO DA CASTELFIORENTINO)

Naturalmente chere ogni amadore
di suo cor la sua donna far saccente,
e questo per la visïon presente
intese di mostrare a te l'Amore

in ciò che de lo tuo ardente core   5
pascëa la tua donna umilemente,
che lungamente stata era dormente,
involta in drappo, d'ogne pena fore.

6a

What you saw, I think, was all nobility and all joy and all the good that man can know; since that great lord was proving his power over you, who is lord of the world of honour: for where he dwells tedium and trouble die, and he holds court in the keep of the mind; and so softly does he come during sleep that he takes men's hearts away without pain.

He took your heart away, seeing that your lady was sinking towards death; and it was because he feared this that he gave it her to eat. And when you saw him leave in sorrow, this was the moment when your sweet sleep was ending, being overcome by its contrary.

6b

REPLY OF CINO DA PISTOIA (OR TERINO DA CASTELFIORENTINO)

It is a law of nature that every lover would have his lady know his heart, and it was this that Love meant to show you with your vision, inasmuch as he humbly fed your lady with your burning heart—she having been asleep for a long while, wrapped in a cloth, away from all distress.

Allegro si mostrò Amor, venendo
a te per darti ciò che 'l cor chiedea, 10
insieme due coraggi comprendendo;

e l'amorosa pena conoscendo
che ne la donna conceputo avea,
per pietà di lei pianse partendo.

6*c* (B. IV)

RISPOSTA DI DANTE DA MAIANO

Di ciò che stato sei dimandatore,
guardando, ti rispondo brevemente,
amico meo di poco canoscente,
mostrandoti del ver lo suo sentore.

Al tuo mistier così son parlatore: 5
se san ti truovi e fermo de la mente,
che lavi la tua coglia largamente,
a ciò che stinga e passi lo vapore

lo qual ti fa favoleggiar loquendo;
e se gravato sei d'infertà rea, 10
sol c'hai farneticato, sappie, intendo.

Così riscritto el meo parer ti rendo;
né cangio mai d'esta sentenza mea,
fin che tua acqua al medico no stendo.

7 (B. LXII)

RISPOSTA DI DANTE A IGNOTO RIMATORE

Com più vi fere Amor co' suoi vincastri,
più li vi fate in ubidirlo presto,
ch'altro consiglio, ben lo vi protesto,
non vi si può già dar: chi vuol, l'incastri.

16

Love showed himself as happy, since he came to give you what your heart desired, joining two hearts together; and he wept as he went away, out of pity for her, knowing the pain of love he had brought about in her.

6c

Having considered, my rather ignorant friend, the matter you ask me about, I answer briefly and explain its true significance. With your needs in mind I say this: if you are well and in your right mind, give your testicles a good wash, so that the vapours that make you talk nonsense be extinguished and dispersed; but if you are suffering from a serious illness, then, believe me, the only thing I understand from your words is that you were raving. Such is my opinion, duly returned; nor will I ever alter my judgement without first showing your water to a doctor.

7

DANTE TO AN UNKNOWN POET

The more Love strikes you with his rods, the more dispose yourself to obey him promptly; for I declare that no other advice can be given you: let him take this who will! Then when the time is ripe, with gentle poultices

Poi, quando fie stagion, coi dolci impiastri   5
farà stornarvi ogni tormento agresto,
ché 'l mal d'Amor non è pesante il sesto
ver ch'è dolce lo ben. Dunque, ormai lastri

vostro cor lo cammin per seguitare
lo suo sommo poder, se v'ha sì punto   10
come dimostra 'l vostro buon trovare;

e non vi disvïate da lui punto,
ch'elli sol può tutt'allegrezza dare
e' suoi serventi meritare a punto.

8 (B. XLVIII)

Se Lippo amico se' tu che mi leggi,
davanti che proveggi
a le parole che dir ti prometto,
da parte di colui che mi t'ha scritto
in tua balia mi metto   5
e recoti salute quali eleggi.

Per tuo onor audir prego mi deggi
e con l'udir richeggi
ad ascoltar la mente e lo 'ntelletto:
io che m'appello umile sonetto,   10
davanti al tuo cospetto
vegno, perché al non caler [non] feggi.

Lo qual ti guido esta pulcella nuda,
che ven di dietro a me sì vergognosa,
ch'a torno gir non osa,   15
perch'ella non ha vesta in che si chiuda;

18

he will cause all harsh pain to leave you; for the suffering brought by Love is outweighed six times over by the sweetness of his joy. Therefore, let your heart pave the road along which to follow after his high majesty—if he has pierced you as much as the excellence of your poem shows. And do not turn one inch aside from his path, for he alone can give all bliss and perfectly reward his servants.

8

TO LIPPO, TO INTRODUCE THE FOLLOWING POEM

If you who read me are friend Lippo, then, before you consider the words I promise to say, I place myself in your keeping with such greeting as you like best, on behalf of him who has written me for you. I beg you, as a gentleman, to hear me; and while you hear, to invite your mind too and intelligence to listen. A humble sonnet I call myself, and I come right into your sight to prevent you ignoring me.

I bring you this naked maiden who is following me all timidly and who dares not walk abroad, for she has no clothes to cover her: and I beg the gentle heart that

e priego il gentil cor che 'n te riposa
che la rivesta e tegnala per druda,
sì che sia conosciuda
e possa andar là 'vunque è disïosa.   20

9 (B. XLIX)

Lo meo servente core   A
vi raccomandi Amor, [che] vi l'ha dato,   G
e Merzé d'altro lato   B
di me vi rechi alcuna rimembranza;   C
   ché, del vostro valore   A   5
avanti ch'io mi sia guari allungato,   B
mi tien già confortato   b
di ritornar la mia dolce speranza.   c
   Deo, quanto fïe poca addimoranza,   C
secondo il mio parvente!   D   10
ché mi volge sovente   D
la mente   per mirar vostra sembianza: C
per che ne lo meo gire e addimorando,
gentil mia donna, a voi mi raccomando.

10 (B. V)

O voi che per la via d'Amor passate,
attendete e guardate
s'elli è dolore alcun, quanto 'l mio, grave;
e prego sol ch'audir mi sofferiate,
e poi imaginate   5
s'io son d'ogni tormento ostale e chiave.

Amor, non già per mia poca bontate,
ma per sua nobiltate,
mi pose in vita sì dolce e soave,
ch'io mi sentia dir dietro spesse fiate: 10
'Deo, per qual dignitate
così leggiadro questi lo core have?'

dwells in you to clothe her and keep her as your friend; so that she may become known and be able to go wherever she pleases.

9

May Love commend to you my loyal heart—Love who gave it to you; and may Kindness, on your other side, remind you sometimes of me: for now, even before I'm far away from your goodness, already a sweet hope of returning consoles me. Ah, how short, it seems to me, will be my sojourn away from you! For memory often makes me turn to gaze at your image. And so, my gentle lady, I commend myself to you, both while on my journey and all the time I am away.

10

O you who pass by on Love's way, attend and consider whether there be any sorrow as heavy as mine: and all I ask is that you hear me patiently, and then see for yourselves how I am the abode and key of all torments. Love —not on account of my slight worth but of his own perfection—placed me in a way of life so sweet and serene that often I would hear people say behind me: 'Heavens, what has he done to deserve having a heart so glad?'

Or ho perduta tutta mia baldanza,
che si movea d'amoroso tesoro;
ond'io pover dimoro,   15
in guisa che di dir mi ven dottanza.

Sì che volendo far come coloro
che per vergogna celan lor mancanza,
di fuor mostro allegranza,
e dentro da lo core struggo e ploro.   20

II (B.VI)

Piangete, amanti, poi che piange Amore,
udendo qual cagion lui fa plorare.
Amor sente a Pietà donne chiamare,
mostrando amaro duol per li occhi fore,

perché villana Morte in gentil core   5
ha miso il suo crudele adoperare,
guastando ciò che al mondo è da laudare
in gentil donna sovra de l'onore.

Audite quanto Amor le fece orranza,
ch'io 'l vidi lamentare in forma vera   10
sovra la morta imagine avvenente;

e riguardava ver lo ciel sovente,
ove l'alma gentil già locata era,
che donna fu di sì gaia sembianza.

12 (B.VII)

Morte villana, di pietà nemica,
di dolor madre antica,
giudicio incontastabile gravoso,
poi che hai data matera al cor doglioso
ond'io vado pensoso,   5
di te blasmar la lingua s'affatica.

Now I have lost all the elation that love's treasure brought me, so that I am left poverty-stricken, even to the point of being afraid to write. Hence, choosing to act like those who for shame conceal their lack of something, I outwardly show joy but in my heart I pine and weep.

II

Lovers, weep because Love weeps; weep to hear why he weeps. Love hears ladies calling on Pity, showing bitter grief through their eyes; because brutal Death has done his cruel work in a gentle heart, destroying that which, besides honour, is praiseworthy in a gentle lady in this world.

Hear the great honour Love did her! For I saw him in his true form lamenting over the lovely dead image; and he looked often towards heaven, where the noble soul had already taken her place, that had been a lady of such charm.

12

Brutal Death, foe of compassion, ancient mother of grief, harsh irreversible doom! Because you have put into my sad heart the cause of my sorrow, my tongue strives to

E s'io di grazia ti vòi far mendica,
convenesi ch'eo dica
lo tuo fallar d'onni torto tortoso,
non però ch'a la gente sia nascoso,   10
ma per farne cruccioso
chi d'amor per innanzi si notrica.

Dal secolo hai partita cortesia
e ciò ch'è in donna da pregiar vertute:
in gaia gioventute   15
distrutta hai l'amorosa leggiadria.

Più non vòi discovrir qual donna sia
che per le propietà sue canosciute.
Chi non merta salute
non speri mai d'aver sua compagnia.   20

13 (B.L)

La dispietata mente, che pur mira
di retro al tempo che se n'è andato,
da l'un dei lati mi combatte il core;
    e 'l disio amoroso, che mi tira
ver lo dolce paese c'ho lasciato,   5
d'altra part'è con la forza d'Amore;
    né dentro i' sento tanto di valore,
che lungiamente i' possa far difesa,
gentil madonna, se da voi non vene:
però, se a voi convene   10
ad iscampo di lui mai fare impresa,
piacciavi di mandar vostra salute,
che sia conforto de la sua virtute.

24

defame you. But if I want to make you detested I must declare your offence, evil with all evils as it is—not that it's concealed from people, but in order to rouse anger against it in anyone who in future may draw nourishment from love.

You have robbed this world of courtesy and of whatever is reputed virtue in woman; you have destroyed lovable charm while still in lighthearted youth. Who the lady was I will not disclose, except by thus naming her known qualities. Let no one who does not merit salvation ever hope to be of her company.

13

1. Pitiless memory, ever gazing back at the time that is past, assails my heart on the one side; on the other, with the power of Love, is the love-longing that draws me towards the dear place which I have left. Nor, gentle lady, do I feel that I have the power in me to resist for long, unless such power come from you; hence if it is fitting that you sometimes take action to rescue my heart, send your greeting, I beg you, to restore its strength.

Piacciavi, donna mia, non venir meno
a questo punto al cor che tanto v'ama,
poi sol da voi lo suo soccorso attende:
  ché buon signor già non ristringe freno
per soccorrer lo servo quando 'l chiama,
ché non pur lui, ma suo onor difende.
  E certo la sua doglia più m'incende,
quand'i' mi penso ben, donna, che vui
per man d'Amor là entro pinta sete:
  così e voi dovete
vie maggiormente aver cura di lui;
ché que' da cui convien che 'l ben s'appari,
per l'imagine sua ne tien più cari.

  Se dir voleste, dolce mia speranza,
di dare indugio a quel ch'io vi domando,
sacciate che l'attender io non posso;
  ch'i' sono al fine de la mia possanza.
E ciò conoscer voi dovete, quando
l'ultima speme a cercar mi son mosso:
  ché tutti incarchi sostenere a dosso
de' l'uomo infin al peso ch'è mortale,
prima che 'l suo maggiore amico provi,
  poi non sa qual lo trovi:
e s'elli avven che li risponda male,
cosa non è che costi tanto cara,
ché morte n'ha più tosto e più amara.

  E voi pur sete quella ch'io più amo,
e che far mi potete maggior dono,
e 'n cui la mia speranza più riposa:
  che sol per voi servir la vita bramo,
e quelle cose che a voi onor sono
dimando e voglio; ogni altra m'è noiosa.

2. I beg you, my lady, do not fail in this emergency the heart that loves you so, since from you alone does it look for help. A good lord will not draw rein when riding to the help of the servant who calls on him; it is not only the latter he thus defends, but his own honour as well. And certainly my heart's pain burns me the more when I consider, lady, that you are depicted therein by the hand of Love: which is a reason for your caring the more for it, if He who is the norm of all goodness holds us the dearer for being made in His image.

3. Were you to say, my sweet hope, that you will make me wait for what I ask of you, know that I cannot wait— I am at the end of my strength. And this you ought to recognize, since it is my last hope that I have begun to look to now: for a man ought to sustain every burden, short of such as would kill him, before appealing to his best friend, since he does not know how his friend may be disposed; and should the response be unkind, then nothing could be bought at greater cost—he will die of it, and the more swiftly and bitterly.

4. And you, yes you, are the one I love above all, and who can make me the greatest gift of all, and in whom above all my hope dwells: and it is only to serve you that I desire life, and I ask and desire only that which may be to your honour—all else is wearisome. You can give me

Dar mi potete ciò ch'altri non m'osa,
ché 'l sì e 'l no di me in vostra mano
ha posto Amore; ond'io grande mi tegno.
La fede ch'eo v'assegno
muove dal portamento vostro umano;   50
ché ciascun che vi mira, in veritate
di fuor conosce che dentro è pietate.

Dunque vostra salute omai si mova,
e vegna dentro al cor, che lei aspetta,
gentil madonna, come avete inteso: 55
    ma sappia che l'entrar di lui si trova
serrato forte da quella saetta
ch'Amor lanciò lo giorno ch'i' fui preso;
    per che l'entrare a tutt'altri è conteso,
fuor ch'a' messi d'Amor, ch'aprir lo sanno   60
per volontà de la vertù che 'l serra:
onde ne la mia guerra
la sua venuta mi sarebbe danno,
sed ella fosse sanza compagnia
de' messi del signor che m'ha in balia.   65

Canzone, il tuo cammin vuol esser corto:
ché tu sai ben che poco tempo omai
puote aver luogo quel per che tu vai.

14 (B.LI)

Non mi poriano già mai fare ammenda
del lor gran fallo gli occhi miei, sed elli
non s'accecasser, poi la Garisenda
torre miraro co' risguardi belli,

e non conobber quella (mal lor prenda!)   5
ch'è la maggior de la qual si favelli:
però ciascun di lor vòi che m'intenda
che già mai pace non farò con elli;

what no one else can, for Love has put into your hands the power of life and death over me, and in this I glory. The trust I place in you comes from the human kindness that shows in you; for everyone who looks at you knows with certainty from your outward bearing that compassion dwells within you.

5. Therefore let your greeting now come forth, and come into my heart that awaits it, my gentle lady, as you have heard. Only let it know that my heart's entrance is securely locked by that arrow which Love shot on the day that I was taken; so that entrance is denied to all except the messengers of Love—they can open it by will of the Power that keeps it locked: hence, tormented as I am, the arrival of your greeting would only harm me should it not be accompanied by the messengers of the Lord who has me in his power.

Congedo. Song, you must travel swiftly, for you know well that there is little time left now to bring about what you are going for.

14

Never can my eyes make amends to me—short of going blind—for their great fault, that they gazed at the Garisenda tower with its fine view, and—confound them!—missed her, the worthiest of those who are talked about. So I want both of them to understand that I'll never make peace with them, since they were capable of seeing

poi tanto furo, che ciò che sentire
doveano a ragion senza veduta,
non conobber vedendo; onde dolenti

10

son li miei spirti per lo lor fallire,
e dico ben, se 'l voler non mi muta,
ch'eo stesso li uccidrò que' scanoscenti!

15 (B.LII)

DANTE A GUIDO CAVALCANTI

Guido, i' vorrei che tu e Lapo ed io
fossimo presi per incantamento
e messi in un vasel, ch'ad ogni vento
per mare andasse al voler vostro e mio,

sì che fortuna od altro tempo rio

5

non ci potesse dare impedimento,
anzi, vivendo sempre in un talento,
di stare insieme crescesse 'l disio.

E monna Vanna e monna Lagia poi
con quella ch'è sul numer de le trenta

10

con noi ponesse il buono incantatore:

e quivi ragionar sempre d'amore,
e ciascuna di lor fosse contenta,
sì come i' credo che saremmo noi.

15a (B.LIII)

RISPOSTA DI GUIDO CAVALCANTI

S'io fosse quelli che d'amor fu degno,
del qual non trovo sol che rimembranza,
e la donna tenesse altra sembianza,
assai mi piaceria siffatto legno.

0

without recognizing what they ought to have been aware of without seeing. So my spirits are sad at their offence and I repeat that—unless I change my mind—I myself will kill them, the dull fools!

15

Guido, I wish that you and Lapo and I could be taken by magic and placed in a boat that, whatever the wind, was carried over the sea wherever you and I chose to go, unhindered by tempest or any foul weather—our desire to be together in fact always increasing, living as we would in unceasing harmony.

And with this, that the good wizard should give us for company lady Vanna and lady Lagia and her who stands on number thirty, there to talk always of love; and that each of them should be happy, as I'm sure we would be.

15*a*

GUIDO CAVALCANTI'S REPLY

If I still were he who was once found worthy of love—him whom now I only remember—and if my lady's looks were different, then a boat like that would please me

E tu, che se' de l'amoroso regno   5
là onde di merzé nasce speranza,
riguarda se 'l mi' spirito ha pesanza:
ch'un prest' arcier di lui ha fatto segno

e tragge l'arco, che li tese Amore,
sì lietamente, che la sua persona   10
par che di gioco porti signoria.

Or odi maraviglia ch'el disia:
lo spirito fedito li perdona,
vedendo che li strugge il suo valore.

16 (B.LXI)

Sonar bracchetti, e cacciatori aizzare,
lepri levare, ed isgridar le genti,
e di guinzagli uscir veltri correnti,
per belle piagge volgere e imboccare,

assai credo che deggia dilettare   5
libero core e van d'intendimenti!
Ed io, fra gli amorosi pensamenti,
d'uno sono schernito in tale affare,

e dicemi esto motto per usanza:
'Or ecco leggiadria di gentil core,   10
per una sì selvaggia dilettanza

lasciar le donne e lor gaia sembianza!'
Allor, temendo non che senta Amore,
prendo vergogna, onde mi ven pesanza.

greatly. But you who belong to Love's kingdom, there where hope of requital is born, consider how my spirit is burdened; for a ready archer has made it his target, and shoots from the bow which Love strung for him so cheerfully that he appears entirely joyful. And now hear the strange thing my spirit desires—stricken, it forgives him, while seeing itself undone by him!

16

The belling of hounds, the cries of hunters urging them on, hares running from cover, the shouting of onlookers, swift greyhounds slipping from the leash, their veering through fair meadows, their snatching the prey—such things must greatly delight, I think, a heart that is free and void of love. But I, taken up with thoughts of love, find myself mocked on this account by one of them who is wont to tease me thus: O what gallantry in a gentleman! For so rough a sport to leave the ladies and their charming ways! Then, fearing that Love may overhear, I grow ashamed and so become heavy-hearted.

17 (B.LIX)

Volgete li occhi a veder chi mi tira,
per ch'i' non posso più venir con vui,
e onoratel, ché questi è colui
che per le gentil donne altrui martira.

La sua vertute, ch'ancide sanz'ira, 5
pregatel che mi laghi venir pui;
ed io vi dico, de li modi sui
cotanto intende quanto l'om sospira:

ch'elli m'è giunto fero ne la mente,
e pingevi una donna sì gentile, 10
che tutto mio valore a' piè le corre;

e fammi udire una voce sottile
che dice: 'Dunque vuo' tu per nëente
a li occhi tuoi sì bella donna tòrre?'

18 (B.LX)

Deh, ragioniamo insieme un poco, Amore,
e tra'mi d'ira, che mi fa pensare;
e se vuol l'un de l'altro dilettare,
trattiam di nostra donna omai, signore.

Certo il vïaggio ne parrà minore 5
prendendo un così dolze tranquillare,
e già mi par gioioso il ritornare,
audendo dire e dir di suo valore.

Or incomincia, Amor, ché si convene,
e moviti a far ciò ch'è la cagione 10
che ti dichini a farmi compagnia,

o vuol merzede o vuol tua cortesia;
ché la mia mente il mio penser dipone,
cotal disio de l'ascoltar mi vene.

17

Turn your eyes to see who it is who draws me so that I can come no further with you; and honour him, for he is the one who brings suffering through gentle ladies. Pray to him that he may allow that power of his, which kills without wrath, to come into me; and I tell you that one understands his ways only in the degree that one sighs.

For he has come fiercely into my mind and he there depicts a lady so noble that all my strength runs to kneel at her feet: and he makes me hear a soft voice saying: 'Will you for a mere nothing withdraw your eyes from so fair a lady?'

18

Come, Love, let's talk together a little, and lift me out of the gloom that saddens my thoughts: and so that each of us take delight in the other, my lord, let our talk be about our lady. The journey will certainly seem shorter if we pass the time thus sweetly; and already my return comes with joy into my mind as I hear you recite her excellence.

Begin now, Love—as you should—begin to do what has led you to deign to keep me company, whether for any merit of mine or from your courtesy: see, my mind lays aside its heavy thoughts, so keen a desire to listen comes over me.

19 <small>(B.LXIII)</small>

Sonetto, se Meuccio t'è mostrato,
così tosto 'l saluta come 'l vedi,
e va' correndo e gittaliti a' piedi,
sì che tu paie bene accostumato.

E quando se' con lui un poco stato,   5
anche 'l risalutrai, non ti ricredi;
e poscia a l'ambasciata tua procedi,
ma fa' che 'l tragghe prima da un lato;

e di': 'Meuccio, que' che t'ama assai
de le sue gioie più care ti manda,   10
per accontarsi al tu' coraggio bono.'

Ma fa' che prenda per lo primo dono
questi tuo' frati, e a lor sì comanda
che stean con lui e qua non tornin mai.

20 <small>(B.VIII)</small>

Cavalcando l'altr'ier per un cammino,
pensoso de l'andar che mi sgradia,
trovai Amore in mezzo de la via
in abito leggier di peregrino.

Ne la sembianza mi parea meschino,   5
come avesse perduto segnoria;
e sospirando pensoso venia,
per non veder la gente, a capo chino.

Quando mi vide, mi chiamò per nome,
e disse: 'Io vegno di lontana parte,   10
ov'era lo tuo cor per mio volere;

e recolo a servir novo piacere.'
Allora presi di lui sì gran parte,
ch'elli disparve, e non m'accorsi come.

19

Sonnet, when Meuccio has been pointed out to you greet him as soon as you see him, and run and throw yourself at his feet—that will show you know how to behave. And when you have been with him a little while, greet him once more—don't be ashamed; then proceed to your mission, but first drawing him aside, and say: 'Meuccio, he who is very fond of you sends you some of the things he counts most precious, so as to win a way into your good heart.' But get him to accept as a first gift these brothers of yours: and tell them to stay with him and never come back.

20

Riding along a road the other day, and brooding over my journey which I disliked, I found Love in my path, meanly dressed like a pilgrim. In his looks he seemed downcast as though he had lost authority; and he came along pensive and sighing, with his head bowed so as not to see anyone.

Seeing me, he called me by name and said: 'I come from far away, where your heart was, in accordance with my will; and I bring it with me to serve another beauty.' Then, I took so much from him that he disappeared— I didn't see how.

21 (B.LVI)

Per una ghirlandetta
ch'io vidi, mi farà
sospirare ogni fiore.

   I' vidi a voi, donna, portare
ghirlandetta di fior gentile,   5
   e sovr'a lei vidi volare
un angiolel d'amore umile;
   e 'n suo cantar sottile
dicea: 'Chi mi vedrà
lauderà 'l mio signore.'   10

   Se io sarò là dove sia
Fioretta mia bella [a sentire],
   allor dirò la donna mia
che port' in testa i miei sospire.
   Ma per crescer disire   15
mïa donna verrà
coronata da Amore.

   Le parolette mie novelle,
che di fiori fatto han ballata,
   per leggiadria ci hanno tolt'elle   20
una vesta ch'altrui fu data:
   però siate pregata,
qual uom la canterà,
che li facciate onore.

22 (B.LVII)

Madonna, quel signor che voi portate   A
ne gli occhi, tal che vince ogni possanza,   B
mi dona sicuranza   B
che voi sarete amica di pietate;   A

38

21

Because of a garland I saw, every flower will make me sigh.

1. Lady, I saw you wearing a garland of sweet flowers, and over it a little angel hovering, a gentle angel of love, who said in his delicate song: 'Whoever sees me will praise my Lord.'

2. When I am where my fair Fioretta may hear me, I will say that my lady wears my sighs around her head. But my lady will come crowned by Love, to increase desire.

3. These new little verses of mine, which have made a ballata of flowers, have taken, to adorn themselves, a garment given to another: so I pray you, lady, be gracious to whoever sings them.

22

Lady, that Lord you bear in your eyes in such a way that he overcomes all resistance, gives me assurance that

però che là dov'ei fa dimoranza,   5
ed ha in compagnia molta beltate,
tragge tutta bontate
a sé, come principio c'ha possanza.
   Ond'io conforto sempre mia speranza,
la qual è stata tanto combattuta,   10
che sarebbe perduta,
se non fosse che Amore
contro ogni avversità le dà valore
   con la sua vista e con la rimembranza
del dolce loco e del soave fiore   15
che di novo colore
cerchiò la mente mia,
merzé di vostra grande cortesia.

23 (B.LVIII)

Deh, Vïoletta, che in ombra d'Amore
ne gli occhi miei sì subito apparisti,
aggi pietà del cor che tu feristi,
che spera in te e disïando more.

   Tu, Vïoletta, in forma più che umana,   5
foco mettesti dentro in la mia mente
col tuo piacer ch'io vidi;
   poi con atto di spirito cocente
creasti speme, che in parte mi sana
là dove tu mi ridi.   10
   Deh, non guardare perché a lei mi fidi,
ma drizza li occhi al gran disio che m'arde,
ché mille donne già per esser tarde
sentiron pena de l'altrui dolore.

you'll be a friend to kindness; for there where he dwells, with great beauty for company, he draws to himself all goodness, mighty principle that he is. So I give new heart to my hope, which has been so much assailed that it would by now have been destroyed but that Love gives it strength against all adversity, with the sight of himself and with the memory of the dear place and of the lovely flower which has ringed my mind with fresh colours, thanks to your great courtesy.

23

Ah, Violetta, you who so suddenly appeared to my eyes in Love's shadow, pity the heart that puts its trust in you and is dying of desire.

You, Violetta, in a more than human form, you kindled a fire in my mind through the beauty that I saw; and then, by the action of a fiery spirit, you quickened a hope that partly heals me when you smile at me. Ah, do not heed my trusting in this hope, but consider rather the great desire that burns me: for countless ladies, through their slowness to respond, have themselves been tormented because of their lovers' anguish.

Ballata, i' vòi che tu ritrovi Amore,
e con lui vade a madonna davante,
sì che la scusa mia, la qual tu cante,
ragioni poi con lei lo mio segnore.

   Tu vai, ballata, sì cortesemente,   5
che sanza compagnia
dovresti avere in tutte parti ardire;
   ma se tu vuoli andar sicuramente,
retrova l'Amor pria,
ché forse non è bon sanza lui gire;   10
   però che quella che ti dee audire,
sì com'io credo, è ver di me adirata:
se tu di lui non fossi accompagnata,
leggeramente ti faria disnore.

   Con dolze sono, quando se' con lui,   15
comincia este parole,
appresso che averai chesta pietate:
   'Madonna, quelli che mi manda a vui,
quando vi piaccia, vole,
sed elli ha scusa, che la m'intendiate.   20
   Amore è qui, che per vostra bieltate
lo face, come vol, vista cangiare:
dunque perché li fece altra guardare
pensatel voi, da che non mutò 'l core.'

   Dille: 'Madonna, lo suo core è stato   25
con sì fermata fede,
che 'n voi servir l'ha 'mpronto onne pensero:
   tosto fu vostro, e mai non s'è smagato.'
Sed ella non ti crede,
di' che domandi Amor, che sa lo vero: 30

24

Ballata, I want you to seek out Love and go with him before my lady, so that when you have sung my excuses my Lord may expound them.

1. Ballata, your bearing is so courteous that even without escort you should have nothing to fear anywhere. But if you wish to go quite safely, seek out Love first; for perhaps it isn't wise to go without him, since she who is to hear you is, I believe, annoyed with me: were you not accompanied by him she might easily receive you coldly.

2. With sweet melody—once you are with him— begin to speak these words (after pleading for mercy): 'My lady, if it so please you, he who sends me to you begs that, if he has any valid excuse, you would hear it from me. Love is here, Love who, just as he pleases, makes him change countenance by means of your beauty. Judge then for yourself why Love made him look at another—seeing that his heart has not changed.'

3. Tell her: 'Lady, his heart has always been of such steadfast fidelity that his every thought has impelled him to serve you: early was he yours and never has he wavered.' If she doesn't believe you, tell her to ask Love who knows the truth. And finally make this humble plea:

ed a la fine falle umil preghero,
lo perdonare se le fosse a noia,
che mi comandi per messo ch'eo moia,
e vedrassi ubidir ben servidore.

E di' a colui ch'è d'ogni pietà chiave,   35
avante che sdonnei,
che le saprà contar mia ragion bona:
'Per grazia de la mia nota soave
reman tu qui con lei,
e del tuo servo ciò che vuoi ragiona;   40
   e s'ella per tuo prego li perdona,
fa' che li annunzi un bel sembiante pace.'
Gentil ballata mia, quando ti piace,
movi in quel punto che tu n'aggie onore.

25 (B.LXVIII)

Lo doloroso amor che mi conduce
a fin di morte per piacer di quella
che lo mio cor solea tener gioioso,
   m'ha tolto e toglie ciascun dì la luce
che avëan li occhi miei di tale stella,   5
che non credea di lei mai star doglioso:
   e 'l colpo suo c'ho portato nascoso,
omai si scopre per soverchia pena,
la qual nasce del foco
che m'ha tratto di gioco,   10
sì ch'altro mai che male io non aspetto;
e 'l viver mio (omai esser de' poco)
fin a la morte mia sospira e dice:
'Per quella moro c'ha nome Beatrice.'

   Quel dolce nome, che mi fa il cor agro,   15
tutte fïate ch'i' lo vedrò scritto
mi farà nuovo ogni dolor ch'io sento;

if she would rather not forgive, let her command me by a messenger to die, and her servant will show perfect obedience.

4. And—before taking your leave of my lady—say to him who is key of all compassion, to him who will know how to plead my good cause: 'By means of my sweet music, remain here with her and speak as you please of your servant. And if, at your prayer, she does forgive him, see that a gracious countenance declare the pardon.' My gentle ballata, go on your way when you please, choosing a moment when you'll find a welcome.

25

1. The sorrowful love that leads me to final death, at the will of her who used to keep my heart in joy, has withdrawn the light and daily withdraws it more—the light that once my eyes received from a star such that I never thought I would be sad on its account. And the wound I had from it I have kept concealed, but now it shows itself through excessive pain—pain caused by that fire which has drawn me away from happiness, so that now I can expect nothing but torment: and my life—which cannot last long now—sighs as it goes to death, and says: 'Through her I die, whose name is Beatrice.'

2. That sweet name which embitters my heart will renew all the pain I feel whenever I see it written; and

e de la doglia diverrò sì magro
de la persona, e 'l viso tanto afflitto,
che qual mi vederà n'avrà pavento.   20
    E allor non trarrà sì poco vento
che non mi meni, sì ch'io cadrò freddo;
e per tal verrò morto,
e 'l dolor sarà scorto
con l'anima che sen girà sì trista;   25
e sempre mai con lei starà ricolto,
ricordando la gio' del dolce viso,
a che nïente par lo paradiso.

    Pensando a quel che d'Amore ho provato,
l'anima mia non chiede altro diletto,   30
né il penar non cura il quale attende:
    ché, poi che 'l corpo sarà consumato,
se n'anderà l'amor che m'ha sì stretto
con lei a Quel ch'ogni ragione intende;
    e se del suo peccar pace no i rende,   35
partirassi col tormentar ch'è degna;
sì che non ne paventa,
e starà tanto attenta
d'imaginar colei per cui s'è mossa,
che nulla pena avrà ched ella senta;   40
sì che, se 'n questo mondo io l'ho perduto,
Amor ne l'altro men darà trebuto.

    Morte, che fai piacere a questa donna,
per pietà, innanzi che tu mi discigli,
va' da lei, fatti dire   45
perché m'avvien che la luce di quigli
che mi fan tristo, mi sia così tolta:
se per altrui ella fosse ricolta,
falmi sentire, e trarra'mi d'errore,
e assai finirò con men dolore.   50

through sorrow I'll become so wasted in body and woeful in face that any who see me will be struck with fear: and the least breath of wind will sweep me along, until I fall down cold; and so I shall die, and my sorrow will be accompanied by my soul on her sad departure, and will evermore remain closely united with her, while she remembers the joy of the sweet face to which Paradise seems nothing in comparison.

3. Reflecting on my experience of Love, my soul desires no other joy and gives no thought to the torment that she expects; for once the body is worn out, the love that has so gripped me will depart with my soul to Him who hears each man's account; and should He not pardon her sins, she will depart with the torment that she has deserved; but in such a way that she will feel no terror of it—being so absorbed in contemplating the image of her who was the cause of her journey, that whatever her punishment may be she will not feel it. Thus if I have been a loser in this world, Love will recompense me in the other.

Congedo. Death, you who do the will of this lady, for pity's sake, before you destroy me, go to her, make her tell you why the light of those eyes that make me suffer has been withdrawn from me so. If another is receiving it, let me know; deliver me from illusion and I shall die with far less sorrow.

26 (B.X)

Tutti li miei penser parlan d'Amore;
e hanno in lor sì gran varïetate,
ch'altro mi fa voler sua potestate,
altro folle ragiona il suo valore,

altro sperando m'apporta dolzore,   5
altro pianger mi fa spesse fïate:
e sol s'accordano in cherer pietate,
tremando di paura che è nel core.

Ond'io non so da qual matera prenda;
e vorrei dire, e non so ch'io mi dica: 10
così mi trovo in amorosa erranza!

E se con tutti vòi fare accordanza,
convenemi chiamar la mia nemica,
madonna la Pietà, che mi difenda.

27 (B.XI)

Con l'altre donne mia vista gabbate,
e non pensate, donna, onde si mova
ch'io vi rassembri sì figura nova
quando riguardo la vostra beltate.

Se lo saveste, non poria Pietate   5
tener più contra me l'usata prova,
ché Amor, quando sì presso a voi mi trova,
prende baldanza e tanta securtate,

che fere tra' miei spiriti paurosi,
e quale ancide, e qual pinge di fore,   10
sì che solo remane a veder vui:

ond'io mi cangio in figura d'altrui,
ma non sì ch'io non senta bene allore
li guai de li scacciati tormentosi.

26

All my thoughts speak of Love, and they so differ among themselves that one makes me desire his dominion, another argues that it is madness, another with hope brings me joy, another often makes me weep; and they only agree in begging for pity, trembling with the fear that is in my heart.

Hence I don't know which to take as my theme, and I should like to write, but I don't know what—such is my uncertainty with regard to love! And if I would bring them all into harmony, I must call on my enemy, lady Pity, to take my side.

27

With the other ladies you mock at my appearance, and you don't consider, lady, the reason why my aspect seems so strange to you when I gaze at your beauty. Did you know the reason, Pity could not persist in her hard ways towards me; for when Love finds me near you he grows exultant and so assured that he strikes into my terrified spirits, killing this one and driving out that, until he alone remains to gaze at you. Hence I am changed into another's aspect—yet not so that I do not then perfectly hear the wails of the outcast tormented spirits.

28 (B.XII)

Ciò che m'incontra, ne la mente more,
quand'i' vegno a veder voi, bella gioia;
e quand'io vi son presso, i' sento Amore
che dice: 'Fuggi, se 'l perir t'è noia.'

Lo viso mostra lo color del core,   5
che, tramortendo, ovunque pò s'appoia;
e per la ebrïetà del gran tremore
le pietre par che gridin: 'Moia, moia.'

Peccato face chi allora mi vide,
se l'alma sbigottita non conforta,   10
sol dimostrando che di me li doglia,

per la pietà, che 'l vostro gabbo ancide,
la qual si crïa ne la vista morta
de li occhi, c'hanno di lor morte voglia.

29 (B.XIII)

Spesse fïate vegnonmi a la mente
le oscure qualità ch'Amor mi dona,
e venmene pietà, sì che sovente
io dico: 'Lasso, avviene elli a persona?'

ch'Amor m'assale subitanamente,   5
sì che la vita quasi m'abbandona:
campami un spirto vivo solamente,
e que' riman perché di voi ragiona.

Poscia mi sforzo, ché mi voglio atare;
e così smorto, d'onne valor voto,   10
vegno a vedervi, credendo guerire:

e se io levo li occhi per guardare,
nel cor mi si comincia uno tremoto,
che fa de' polsi l'anima partire.

28

All that befalls me when I set out to see you, fair joy, vanishes from memory; but, when I draw close to you I hear Love saying: 'If you would not perish, fly!' My face shows the colour of my heart which, swooning, seeks support wherever it can; and in the whirl of my violent trembling the stones seem to cry out: 'Die! Die!'

Any one who sees me then commits a sin if he does not comfort my bewildered soul, at least by showing that he is sorry for me, with the pity that your mockery kills, the pity that's born of the dead expression of my eyes that desire their death.

29

Often there come to my mind the dark qualities Love gives me, and pity for myself comes over me, so that often I exclaim: 'Alas, does this happen to anyone else?' For Love assails me suddenly, so that life almost leaves me; only one spirit survives in me, and that remains because it speaks of you.

Then I exert myself, desiring to find some remedy, and thus pale and powerless I come to see you, thinking to be cured; but when I lift my eyes to look at you, a trembling begins in my heart which drives the soul away from my blood.

30 (B.LXV)

De gli occhi de la mia donna si move
un lume sì gentil, che dove appare
si veggion cose ch'uom non può ritrare
per loro altezza e per lor esser nove:

e de' suoi razzi sovra 'l meo cor piove   5
tanta paura, che mi fa tremare,
e dicer: 'Qui non voglio mai tornare';
ma poscia perdo tutte le mie prove,

e tornomi colà dov'io son vinto,
riconfortando gli occhi päurusi,   10
che sentier prima questo gran valore.

Quando son giunto, lasso, ed e' son chiusi;
lo disio che li mena quivi è stinto:
però proveggia a lo mio stato Amore.

31 (B.LXVI)

Ne le man vostre, gentil donna mia,
raccomando lo spirito che more:
e' se ne va sì dolente, ch'Amore
lo mira con pietà, che 'l manda via.

Voi lo legaste alla sua signoria,   5
sì che non ebbe poi alcun valore
di poter lui chiamar se non: 'Signore,
qualunque vuoi di me, quel vo' che sia.'

Io so che a voi ogni torto dispiace:
però la morte, che non ho servita,   10
molto più m'entra ne lo core amara.

Gentil mia donna, mentre ho de la vita,
per tal ch'io mora consolato in pace,
vi piaccia a gli occhi mei non esser cara.

30

From my lady's eyes there comes a light so noble that
where it appears things are seen that no one can describe,
so sublime and wonderful they are. And from its rays
such a fear rains down on my heart as makes me tremble
and say: 'Never will I return here.' But then, losing all
power to resist, I return to the place where I am overcome, comforting my frightened eyes which were the
first to feel that great power. When I reach that place,
alas, see, they are forced to close; the desire which
brought them is extinguished there. Let Love then look
to my state!

31

Into your hands, my gentle lady, I commend my dying
spirit: it goes on its way so sadly that Love himself, who
sends it away, regards it with pity. You bound it subject
to his dominion, so that from that moment it was powerless to invoke him save in these words: 'Lord, whatever
be your will in my regard, that is my will also.'

I know that all wrong displeases you; that is why the
death which I have not deserved is the more—far more—
bitter to me as it enters my heart. My gentle lady, while
life is still in me, may it please you, so that I die consoled
and in peace, not to be ungenerous to my eyes.

32 (B.LXVII)

E' m'incresce di me sì duramente,
ch'altrettanto di doglia
mi reca la pietà quanto 'l martiro,
    lasso, però che dolorosamente
sento contro mia voglia   5
raccoglier l'aire del sezza' sospiro
    entro 'n quel cor che i belli occhi feriro
quando li aperse Amor con le sue mani
per conducermi al tempo che mi sface.
Oïmè, quanto piani,   10
soavi e dolci ver me si levaro,
quand'elli incominciaro
la morte mia, che tanto mi dispiace,
dicendo: 'Nostro lume porta pace!'

    'Noi darem pace al core, a voi diletto',   15
diceano a li occhi miei
quei de la bella donna alcuna volta;
    ma poi che sepper di loro intelletto
che per forza di lei
m'era la mente già ben tutta tolta,   20
    con le insegne d'Amor dieder la volta;
sì che la lor vittorïosa vista
poi non si vide pur una fïata:
ond'è rimasa trista
l'anima mia che n'attendea conforto,   25
e ora quasi morto
vede lo core a cui era sposata,
e partir la convene innamorata.

    Innamorata se ne va piangendo
fora di questa vita   30
la sconsolata, ché la caccia Amore.

32

1. I pity myself so intensely that the pity brings me no less pain than my suffering; for painfully, alas, and unwillingly I feel the air of the last sigh gathering in my heart—the heart which the fair eyes smote when Love opened them with his hands to bring me to the moment of my undoing. Alas, how soft, sweet and gentle they were as they lifted towards me, when they began to cause the death that so grieves me, saying: 'Our light brings peace'!

2. 'Peace we'll give to the heart and joy to you,' they said—the eyes of the fair lady—to my eyes on several occasions. But once they knew with their understanding that through her power my mind was now wholly captive, they wheeled about with Love's banners, so that never again, not once, was their victorious aspect seen: hence my soul, which expected consolation from them, is left sorrowful, and now she sees the heart to which she was joined in marriage almost dead, while she must go on her separate way full of love.

3. Full of love and unconsoled she goes off weeping out of this life, for Love drives her away. She starts on

Ella si move quinci sì dolendo,
ch'anzi la sua partita
l'ascolta con pietate il suo fattore.

Ristretta s'è entro il mezzo del core   35
con quella vita che rimane spenta
solo in quel punto ch'ella si va via;
e ivi si lamenta
d'Amor, che fuor d'esto mondo la caccia;
e spessamente abbraccia   40
li spiriti che piangon tuttavia,
però che perdon la lor compagnia.

L'imagine di questa donna siede
su ne la mente ancora,
là 've la pose quei che fu sua guida;   45
e non le pesa del mal ch'ella vede,
anzi, vie più bella ora
che mai e vie più lieta par che rida;
e alza li occhi micidiali, e grida
sopra colei che piange il suo partire: 50
'Vanne, misera, fuor, vattene omai!'
Questo grida il desire
che mi combatte così come sole,
avvegna che men dole,
però che 'l mio sentire è meno assai   55
ed è più presso al terminar de' guai.

Lo giorno che costei nel mondo venne,
secondo che si trova
nel libro de la mente che vien meno,
la mia persona pargola sostenne   60
una passïon nova,
tal ch'io rimasi di paura pieno;
ch'a tutte mie virtù fu posto un freno
subitamente, sì ch'io caddi in terra,
per una luce che nel cuor percosse: 65

56

her journey lamenting so bitterly that before she has yet gone her Maker listens to her with compassion. She has shrunk back into the innermost heart with such life as is extinguished only at the instant of her departure; and there she complains against Love who is driving her out of this world; and embraces again and again the vital spirits who mourn continually the loss of their companion.

4. The image of that lady still reigns up in the mind, where she was placed by him who was her guide; but she cares nothing for the suffering she sees—indeed, much lovelier than ever now and more full of joy, she seems to laugh; and she lifts her death-dealing eyes and cries out in triumph over her who laments at departing: 'Away with you, wretch, away now!' Such is the cry of the one I desire, assailing me as she always did—though now with less pain for me, inasmuch as my power to feel is much diminished now, and is nearer to the end of its sufferings.

5. The day that this lady came into the world—as I find it written in the book of the mind that is passing away—my childish body felt a strange emotion so that I was filled with fear; and suddenly a check was placed on all my faculties, so that I fell to the ground; and if that

e se 'l libro non erra,
lo spirito maggior tremò sì forte,
che parve ben che morte
per lui in questo mondo giunta fosse:
ma or ne incresce a Quei che questo mosse.　　70

　　Quando m'apparve poi la gran biltate
che sì mi fa dolere,
donne gentili a cu' i' ho parlato,
　　quella virtù che ha più nobilitate,
mirando nel piacere,　　　　　　　　　　75
s'accorse ben che 'l suo male era nato;
　　e conobbe 'l disio ch'era creato
per lo mirare intento ch'ella fece;
sì che piangendo disse a l'altre poi:
'Qui giugnerà, in vece　　　　　　　　80
d'una ch'io vidi, la bella figura,
che già mi fa paura;
che sarà donna sopra tutte noi,
tosto che fia piacer de li occhi suoi.'

　　Io ho parlato a voi, giovani donne,　　85
che avete li occhi di bellezze ornati
e la mente d'amor vinta e pensosa,
perché raccomandati
vi sian li detti miei ovunque sono:
e 'nnanzi a voi perdono　　　　　　　90
la morte mia a quella bella cosa
che me n'ha colpa e mai non fu pietosa.

33 (B.XIV)

Donne ch'avete intelletto d'amore,
i' vo' con voi de la mia donna dire,
non perch'io creda sua laude finire,
ma ragionar per isfogar la mente.

book does not err, the greater spirit then trembled so violently it seemed just as if death had entered this world to take it. But now He who set this world in motion Himself has pity on it.

6. And then—gentle ladies to whom all this is said—when the great beauty which causes me so much suffering appeared to me, that faculty which is noblest, gazing into the beauty, saw that its own suffering was born, and recognized the desire that was caused by its own intense gazing; so that weeping it then said to the other faculties: 'Here, representing one whom I have seen, will come as soon as it pleases her eyes, the beautiful image which already affects me with fear and which will rule as mistress over us all.'

Congedo. It is to you I have spoken, young ladies who have eyes adorned with beauty and minds overcome and troubled by love, to commend my poem to you wherever it may go: and in your presence I pardon that fair one for my death—she who's to blame for it, who has never shown compassion.

33

1. Ladies who have understanding of love, I wish to speak with you of my lady; not that I think I can exhaust her praises, but I want to speak to unburden my mind.

Io dico che pensando il suo valore,　　　　5
Amor sì dolce mi si fa sentire,
che s'io allora non perdessi ardire,
farei parlando innamorar la gente.
　E io non vo' parlar sì altamente,
ch'io divenisse per temenza vile;　　　　10
ma tratterò del suo stato gentile
a respetto di lei leggeramente,
donne e donzelle amorose, con vui,
ché non è cosa da parlarne altrui.

　Angelo clama in divino intelletto　　　　15
e dice: 'Sire, nel mondo si vede
maraviglia ne l'atto che procede
d'un'anima che 'nfin qua su risplende.'
　Lo cielo, che non have altro difetto
che d'aver lei, al suo segnor la chiede,　　　　20
e ciascun santo ne grida merzede.
Sola Pietà nostra parte difende,
　che parla Dio, che di madonna intende:
'Diletti miei, or sofferite in pace
che vostra spene sia quanto me piace　　　　25
là 'v'è alcun che perder lei s'attende,
e che dirà ne lo inferno: "O mal nati,
io vidi la speranza de' beati".'

　Madonna è disïata in sommo cielo:
or vòi di sua virtù farvi savere.　　　　30
Dico, qual vuol gentil donna parere
vada con lei, che quando va per via,
　gitta nei cor villani Amore un gelo,
per che onne lor pensero agghiaccia e pere;
e qual soffrisse di starla a vedere　　　　35
diverria nobil cosa, o si morria.

I say that when I consider her perfection Love makes himself felt in me so sweetly that, did I not then lose courage, I would make people in love with her by speech alone. However, I will not attempt a style so lofty as to make me faint-hearted through fear; rather, I will speak of her excellence in a meagre style—compared with what she is—and to you, ladies and girls who know love; for it is not a thing to speak of to others.

2. An angel cries in the divine intellect, saying: 'Lord, in the world there appears a marvel in act, proceeding from a soul whose splendour reaches even here on high!' Heaven, whose only lack is the lack of her, begs her from its Lord, and every saint cries out for this favour. Pity alone defends our cause, so that God, his mind on my lady, says: 'My loved ones, bear it patiently that your hope remains as long as I please in the place where there is one who knows he will lose her, and who in hell will declare: "O ill-fated ones, I have seen the hope of the blessed"'.

3. My lady is desired in highest heaven: and now I wish to show you something of her excellence. I say that any lady who would show she is noble should go in her company; for when she passes on her way Love casts a chill on base hearts, so that every thought in them freezes and dies; and were any such person able to stay and regard her, he would either become noble or die. And

E quando trova alcun che degno sia
di veder lei, quei prova sua vertute,
ché li avvien, ciò che li dona, in salute,
e sì l'umilia, ch'ogni offesa oblia.   40
Ancor l'ha Dio per maggior grazia dato
che non pò mal finir chi l'ha parlato.

Dice di lei Amor: 'Cosa mortale
come esser pò sì adorna e sì pura?'
Poi la reguarda, e fra se stesso giura   45
che Dio ne 'ntenda di far cosa nova.
Color di perle ha quasi, in forma quale
convene a donna aver, non for misura:
ella è quanto de ben pò far natura;
per essemplo di lei bieltà si prova.   50
De li occhi suoi, come ch'ella li mova,
escono spirti d'amore inflammati,
che feron li occhi a qual che allor la guati,
e passan sì che 'l cor ciascun retrova:
voi le vedete Amor pinto nel viso,   55
là 've non pote alcun mirarla fiso.

Canzone, io so che tu girai parlando
a donne assai, quand'io t'avrò avanzata.
Or t'ammonisco, perch'io t'ho allevata
per figliuola d'Amor giovane e piana,   60
che là 've giugni tu diche pregando:
'Insegnatemi gir, ch'io son mandata
a quella di cui laude so' adornata.'
E se non vuoli andar sì come vana,
non restare ove sia gente villana: 65
ingegnati, se puoi, d'esser palese
solo con donne o con omo cortese,
che ti merranno là per via tostana.
Tu troverai Amor con esso lei;
raccomandami a lui come tu dei.   70

when she finds someone worthy to see her, he receives the full effect of her power; for what she then gives him turns to his good and happiness, and renders him so humble that he forgets every injury. Again, God has given her this greater grace, that no one who has spoken with her can come to an evil end.

4. Love says of her: 'How can a mortal creature be so lovely and so pure?' Then he looks at her and swears within himself that in making her God intends to make a marvel. Her colour is pearl-like, in a way befitting a lady, not to excess. She is the most perfect thing that Nature can produce: beauty is known as imaged in her. From her eyes, wherever she turns them, come fiery spirits of love that strike the eyes of whoever may be regarding her, and pass inward so that each one reaches the heart: you see Love depicted in her face, there where no one can fix his gaze.

Congedo. Song, I know that when I've sent you forth you will go about speaking to many ladies. Now I charge you—having brought you up to be a modest young daughter of Love—that wherever you come you make this request: 'Tell me where I am to go, for I have been sent to her with whose praises I am adorned.' And if you don't wish to travel in vain, don't stop where there are base people; contrive, if you can, to show yourself only to ladies or men of courteous mind, who will lead you quickly to your destination. With her you will find Love; commend me to him, as is your duty.

34 (B. XVI)

Amore e 'l cor gentil sono una cosa,
sì come il saggio in suo dittare pone,
e così esser l'un sanza l'altro osa
com'alma razional sanza ragione.

Falli natura quand'è amorosa,   5
Amor per sire e 'l cor per sua magione,
dentro la qual dormendo si riposa
tal volta poca e tal lunga stagione.

Bieltate appare in saggia donna pui,
che piace a li occhi sì, che dentro al core   10
nasce un disio de la cosa piacente;

e tanto dura talora in costui,
che fa svegliar lo spirito d'Amore.
E simil face in donna omo valente.

35 (B. XVII)

Ne li occhi porta la mia donna Amore,
per che si fa gentil ciò ch'ella mira;
ov'ella passa, ogn'om ver lei si gira,
e cui saluta fa tremar lo core,

sì che, bassando il viso, tutto smore,   5
e d'ogni suo difetto allor sospira:
fugge dinanzi a lei superbia ed ira.
Aiutatemi, donne, farle onore.

Ogne dolcezza, ogne pensero umile
nasce nel core a chi parlar la sente,   10
ond'è laudato chi prima la vide.

Quel ch'ella par quando un poco sorride,
non si pò dicer né tenere a mente,
sì è novo miracolo e gentile.

34

Love and the noble heart are one thing, as the wise man states in his poem, and the one can no more exist without the other than a rational soul without reason. Nature creates them when disposed to love—Love as the lord and the heart as his mansion, wherein he lies asleep, sometimes a little and sometimes a long while.

Then beauty appears in a woman worthy of love, beauty that so pleases the eyes that in the heart is born a desire for the pleasing object; and the desire sometimes continues there long enough to rouse the spirit of Love. And a like effect is caused in a woman by a worthy man.

35

My lady bears Love in her eyes, so that she ennobles all she looks at. Wherever she goes everyone turns towards her, and when she greets someone she makes his heart tremble, so that, lowering his eyes, he turns all pale and sighs over all his faults. Pride and ill humour fly before her. Help me, ladies, to do her honour.

All gentleness, every humble thought is born in the heart of all who hear her speak; and so he who first sees her is praised. What she seems when she smiles a little can neither be described nor held before the mind; it is a marvel so rare and perfect.

36 (B.XVIII)

Voi che portate la sembianza umile,
con li occhi bassi, mostrando dolore,
onde venite che 'l vostro colore
par divenuto de pietà simile?

Vedeste voi nostra donna gentile   5
bagnar nel viso suo di pianto Amore?
Ditelmi, donne, ché 'l mi dice il core,
perch'io vi veggio andar sanz'atto vile.

E se venite da tanta pietate,
piacciavi di restar qui meco alquanto,   10
e qual che sia di lei, nol mi celate.

Io veggio li occhi vostri c'hanno pianto,
e veggiovi tornar sì sfigurate,
che 'l cor mi triema di vederne tanto.

37 (B. XIX)

'Se' tu colui c'hai trattato sovente
di nostra donna, sol parlando a nui?
Tu risomigli a la voce ben lui,
ma la figura ne par d'altra gente.

E perché piangi tu sì coralmente,   5
che fai di te pietà venire altrui?
Vedestù pianger lei, che tu non pui
punto celar la dolorosa mente?

Lascia piangere noi e triste andare
(e fa peccato chi mai ne conforta),   10
che nel suo pianto l'udimmo parlare.

Ell'ha nel viso la pietà sì scorta,
che qual l'avesse voluta mirare
sarebbe innanzi lei piangendo morta.'

36

You whose looks are lowly, with eyes downcast, showing grief, where do you come from that your colour seems to have become like pity itself? Did you see our gentle lady bathing Love with tears in her eyes? Tell me, ladies, for so my heart tells me, seeing you go by with a bearing quite ennobled.

And if you do come from such grief, please stay here awhile with me, and do not hide from me how it fares with her. I see your eyes that have wept, and I see you return so disfigured that my heart trembles to see even only this.

37

'Are you he who has often written about our lady, addressing us alone? In voice you certainly resemble him, but your aspect seems that of another. And why do you weep so bitterly that you make others feel pity for you? Did you see her weeping that you can conceal none of your inward grief?

Leave it to us to weep and go sadly on our way (and to seek to comfort us would be a sin)—leave it to us who have heard her speaking through her tears. Suffering is so visible in her face that anyone who had ventured to gaze at her would have died of weeping in her presence.'

38 (B.LXX)

Onde venite voi così pensose?
Ditemel, s'a voi piace, in cortesia,
ch'i' ho dottanza che la donna mia
non vi faccia tornar così dogliose.

Deh, gentil donne, non siate sdegnose,   5
né di ristare alquanto in questa via
e dire al doloroso che disia
udir de la sua donna alquante cose,

avvegna che gravoso m'è l'udire:
sì m'ha in tutto Amor da sé scacciato,   10
ch'ogni suo atto mi trae a ferire.

Guardate bene s'i' son consumato,
ch'ogni mio spirto comincia a fuggire,
se da voi, donne, non son confortato.

39 (B.LXXI)

Voi, donne, che pietoso atto mostrate,
chi è esta donna che giace sì venta?
sarebbe quella ch'è nel mio cor penta?
Deh, s'ella è dessa, più non mel celate.

Ben ha le sue sembianze sì cambiate,   5
e la figura sua mi par sì spenta,
ch'al mio parere ella non rappresenta
quella che fa parer l'altre beate.

'Se nostra donna conoscer non pòi,
ch'è sì conquisa, non mi par gran fatto,   10
però che quel medesmo avvenne a noi.

38

Where do you come from so sorrowfully? Tell me please, for courtesy's sake; for I fear it may be my lady who is the cause of your returning so sadly. Ah, gentle ladies, do not disdain to stop a while here in the street and to speak to one who is sad and longs for news of his lady—painful though it may be for me to hear it, now that Love has so spurned me that every action of his is a blow aimed at me. See how worn away I am: if I get no consolation from you, ladies, my spirits will all take flight.

39

Ladies who show pity in your bearing, who is this who lies so prostrate? Is she the one depicted in my heart? Ah, if she is, don't keep it from me. Her appearance is indeed so changed and her face seems so lifeless, that to my thinking she does not resemble the one who makes other women appear blessed.

'If you cannot recognize our lady, she being so overcome, that is no surprise to me, for the same

Ma se tu mirerai il gentil atto
de li occhi suoi, conosceraila poi:
non pianger più, tu se' già tutto sfatto.'

40 (B.XX)

Donna pietosa e di novella etate,
adorna assai di gentilezze umane,
ch'era là 'v'io chiamava spesso Morte,
   veggendo li occhi miei pien di pietate,
e ascoltando le parole vane,   5
si mosse con paura a pianger forte.
   E altre donne, che si fuoro accorte
di me per quella che meco piangia,
fecer lei partir via,
e appressarsi per farmi sentire.   10
Qual dicea: 'Non dormire',
e qual dicea: 'Perché sì ti sconforte?'
Allor lassai la nova fantasia,
chiamando il nome de la donna mia.

   Era la voce mia sì dolorosa   15
e rotta sì da l'angoscia del pianto,
ch'io solo intesi il nome nel mio core;
   e con tutta la vista vergognosa
ch'era nel viso mio giunta cotanto,
mi fece verso lor volgere Amore.   20
   Elli era tale a veder mio colore,
che facea ragionar di morte altrui:
'Deh, consoliam costui',
pregava l'una l'altra umilemente;
e dicevan sovente: 25
'Che vedestù, che tu non hai valore?'
E quando un poco confortato fui,
io dissi: 'Donne, dicerollo a vui.

happened to us. But if you look at the gentle expression of her eyes, you will know her. Don't cry any more; you are already quite worn out.'

40

1. A lady, tender in heart and young, much graced with gentle qualities, who was by me when I was often calling on Death, seeing my eyes full of grief and hearing my wild words, began to weep violently out of fear. And other women, made aware of me by her who was weeping beside me, led her away and themselves drew near to recall me to myself. One said: 'Sleep no more'; another: 'Why are you so distressed?' Then I came out of the strange vision, calling on my lady's name.

2. So grief-stricken was my voice, so broken with the stress of sobbing, that I alone heard that name in my heart; and, notwithstanding the shame that had come over my face, Love turned me towards them. Such was my colour, it made them speak of death. 'Ah, let us comfort him', they gently begged one another; and repeatedly they said: 'What was it you saw that you are left so faint?' And I, when I had recovered a little, said: 'Ladies, I'll tell you.

Mentr'io pensava la mia frale vita,
e vedea 'l suo durar com'è leggiero,   30
piansemi Amor nel core, ove dimora;
   per che l'anima mia fu sì smarrita,
che sospirando dicea nel pensero:
"Ben converrà che la mia donna mora."
   Io presi tanto smarrimento allora,   35
ch'io chiusi li occhi vilmente gravati,
e furon sì smagati
li spirti miei, che ciascun giva errando;
e poscia imaginando,
di caunoscenza e di verità fora,   40
visi di donne m'apparver crucciati,
che mi dicean pur: "Morra'ti, morra'ti."

   Poi vidi cose dubitose molte,
nel vano imaginare ov'io entrai;
ed esser mi parea non so in qual loco,   45
   e veder donne andar per via disciolte,
qual lagrimando, e qual traendo guai,
che di tristizia saettavan foco.
   Poi mi parve vedere a poco a poco
turbar lo sole e apparir la stella,   50
e pianger elli ed ella;
cader li augelli volando per l'are,
e la terra tremare;
ed omo apparve scolorito e fioco,
dicendomi: "Che fai? non sai novella?   55
Morta è la donna tua, ch'era sì bella."

   Levava li occhi miei bagnati in pianti,
e vedea, che parean pioggia di manna,
li angeli che tornavan suso in cielo,
   e una nuvoletta avean davanti,   60
dopo la qual gridavan tutti: *Osanna*;
e s'altro avesser detto, a voi dire'lo.

3. 'While I was thinking of the frailty of my life, and seeing how slight is its power to endure, Love wept in my heart, where he dwells; at which my soul became so dismayed that with sighs I said in my thoughts: "It's true, my lady will have to die." Then such dismay took hold of me that I closed my eyes that were weighed down with despondency; and so distracted were my spirits that each went his way, not knowing where; and then in my fantasy, all lost to knowledge and truth, women's faces loomed angrily at me, repeating these words: "You will die! You will die!"

4. 'Then, in the delusive vision I came into I saw many fearful things; and I seemed to find myself in a strange place and to see dishevelled women going by, some weeping, some uttering laments that were as fiery arrows of sorrow. Then I seemed to see little by little the sun grow dark and the stars come out, both he and they weeping; the birds in full flight fall to the ground and the earth tremble; and a man appeared, pale and faint, who said to me: "What are you doing? Don't you know what has happened? Your lady, who was so beautiful, is dead."

5. 'I raised my eyes, wet with tears, and saw the angels like a shower of manna returning on high to heaven; and a small cloud went before them, and following it they all cried, "Hosannah!"—and if they had said more

Allor diceva Amor: "Più nol ti celo;
vieni a veder nostra donna che giace."
Lo imaginar fallace   65
mi condusse a veder madonna morta;
e quand'io l'avea scorta,
vedea che donne la covrian d'un velo;
ed avea seco umiltà verace,
che parea che dicesse: "Io sono in pace."   70

Io divenia nel dolor sì umile,
veggendo in lei tanta umiltà formata,
ch'io dicea: "Morte, assai dolce ti tegno;
     tu dei omai esser cosa gentile,
poi che tu se' ne la mia donna stata,   75
e dei aver pietate e non disdegno.
     Vedi che sì desideroso vegno
d'esser de' tuoi, ch'io ti somiglio in fede.
Vieni, ché 'l cor te chiede."
Poi mi partia, consumato ogne duolo;   80
e quand'io era solo,
dicea, guardando verso l'alto regno:
"Beato, anima bella, chi te vede!"
Voi mi chiamaste allor, vostra merzede.'

41 (B.LXXII)

Un dì si venne a me Malinconia
e disse: 'Io voglio un poco stare teco';
e parve a me ch'ella menasse seco
Dolore e Ira per sua compagnia.

E io le dissi: 'Partiti, va' via';   5
ed ella mi rispose come un greco:
e ragionando a grande agio meco,
guardai e vidi Amore, che venia

74

I would tell you. Then Love said: "I will hide it from you no longer; come and see our lady where she lies." So the false vision led me to see my lady dead; and when I came in sight of her I saw ladies covering her with a veil; and with her was true humility, such that she seemed to say: "I am in peace."

6. 'In my grief I became so humble, seeing such great humility take form in her, that I said: "Death, I hold you very dear: now you are surely ennobled, since you have been with my lady; you are surely merciful and not harsh. I have become, you see, so full of desire to be yours that truly I have taken on your very likeness. Come, for my heart calls you." Then, all mourning done, I went away; and when I was alone I said, looking up towards the high kingdom: "Blessed is he who sees you, fair soul!" It was then that, in your kindness, you called me.'

41

One day Melancholy came to me and said: 'I want to stay with you awhile'; and it seemed to me she brought Sorrow and Wrath with her as companions. And I said: 'Be off! Away with you!' But she answered like a Greek: and while she continued speaking with me, perfectly at her ease, I looked and saw Love drawing near, dressed in

vestito di novo d'un drappo nero,
e nel suo capo portava un cappello;   10
e certo lacrimava pur di vero.

Ed eo li dissi: 'Che hai, cattivello?'
Ed el rispose: 'Eo ho guai e pensero,
ché nostra donna mor, dolce fratello.'

42 (B.XXI)

Io mi senti' svegliar dentro a lo core
un spirito amoroso che dormia:
e poi vidi venir da lungi Amore
allegro sì, che appena il conoscia,

dicendo: 'Or pensa pur di farmi onore';   5
e 'n ciascuna parola sua ridia.
E poco stando meco il mio segnore,
guardando in quella parte onde venia,

io vidi monna Vanna e monna Bice
venire inver lo loco là 'v'io era,   10
l'una appresso de l'altra maraviglia;

e sì come la mente mi ridice,
Amor mi disse: 'Quell'è Primavera,
e quell'ha nome Amor, sì mi somiglia.'

43 (B.XXII)

Tanto gentile e tanto onesta pare
la donna mia quand'ella altrui saluta,
ch'ogne lingua deven tremando muta,
e li occhi no l'ardiscon di guardare.

a new black cloak, with a hat on his head, and weeping real tears. And I said to him: 'What's the matter, poor fellow?' And he replied: 'I'm troubled and sad, for our lady is dying, dear brother.'

42

I felt a sleeping spirit of love awaken in my heart, and then I saw Love coming from far off, so joyful that I hardly knew him; and he said: 'Now think only of doing me honour'—smiling with every word he spoke. And, my Lord staying a little while with me, I looked in the direction he'd come from, and I saw my lady Vanna and my lady Bice coming towards the place where I was, the one marvel following the other; and as memory now retells it, Love said to me: 'This one is Spring, and the other's name is Love, so much does she resemble me.'

43

So gentle and so full of dignity my lady appears when she greets anyone that all tongues tremble and fall silent and eyes dare not look at her. She goes on her way, hearing

Ella si va, sentendosi laudare,
benignamente d'umiltà vestuta;
e par che sia una cosa venuta
da cielo in terra a miracol mostrare.

Mostrasi sì piacente a chi la mira,
che dà per li occhi una dolcezza al core,
che 'ntender no la può chi no la prova:

e par che de la sua labbia si mova
un spirito soave pien d'amore,
che va dicendo a l'anima: 'Sospira.'

44 (B.XXIII)

Vede perfettamente onne salute
chi la mia donna tra le donne vede;
quelle che vanno con lei son tenute
di bella grazia a Dio render merzede.

E sua bieltate è di tanta vertute,
che nulla invidia a l'altre ne procede,
anzi le face andar seco vestute
di gentilezza, d'amore e di fede.

La vista sua fa onne cosa umile;
e non fa sola sé parer piacente,
ma ciascuna per lei riceve onore.

Ed è ne li atti suoi tanto gentile,
che nessun la si può recare a mente,
che non sospiri in dolcezza d'amore.

herself praised, graciously clothed with humility; and seems a creature come down from heaven to earth to make the miraculous known.

She appears so beautiful to those who gaze at her that through the eyes she sends a sweetness into the heart such as none can understand but he who experiences it; and from her lips seems to come a spirit, gentle and full of love, that says to the soul: 'Sigh.'

44

He perfectly sees all bliss who sees my lady among ladies: the ladies who accompany her are bound to give thanks to God for this lovely grace. And her loveliness is of such power that no envy of it arises in other women; rather it makes them go with her clothed in nobility, love, and constancy.

The sight of her makes every creature humble, and it not only shows her as lovely but through her every woman is honoured. And in her bearing she is so noble that no one can call her to mind without sighing with the sweetness of love.

45 (b.lxix)

Di donne io vidi una gentile schiera
questo Ognissanti prossimo passato,
e una ne venia quasi imprimiera,
veggendosi l'Amor dal destro lato.

De gli occhi suoi gittava una lumera,   5
la qual parea un spirito infiammato;
e i' ebbi tanto ardir, ch'in la sua cera
guarda', [e vidi] un angiol figurato.

A chi era degno donava salute
co gli atti suoi quella benigna e piana,   10
e 'mpiva 'l core a ciascun di vertute.

Credo che de lo ciel fosse soprana,
e venne in terra per nostra salute:
là 'nd'è beata chi l'è prossimana.

46 (b.xxiv)

Sì lungiamente m'ha tenuto Amore
e costumato a la sua segnoria,
che sì com'elli m'era forte in pria,
così mi sta soave ora nel core.
   Però quando mi tolle sì 'l valore,   5
che li spiriti par che fuggan via,
allor sente la frale anima mia
tanta dolcezza, che 'l viso ne smore,
   poi prende Amore in me tanta vertute,
che fa li miei spiriti gir parlando,   10
ed escon for chiamando
la donna mia, per darmi più salute.
Questo m'avvene ovunque ella mi vede,
e sì è cosa umil, che nol si crede.

45

Last All Saints' Day I saw a lovely group of ladies, and one seemed to be at their head, Love being visible at her right hand. From her eyes she cast a light that seemed like a spirit aflame. And I made so bold as to look into her face, and I saw an angel imaged there.

Kindly and gentle, she greeted with voice and gesture those who were worthy of such honour, filling each one's heart with goodness. I believe she was a high being of heaven, come down on earth for our salvation; hence every woman with her is blessed.

46

Love has possessed me so long and so schooled me to his sway, that whereas formerly he was harsh to me, he now dwells gently in my heart. Thus when he so deprives me of strength that my spirits seem to flee away, it is then that my frail soul feels such sweetness that my face turns pale with it; for Love assumes such power within me that he gives my spirits voice to speak as they move, and they come forth calling on my lady, to grant me greater bliss. This happens to me whenever she sees me, and it is a thing so humble it passes belief.

47 (B.XXV)

Li occhi dolenti per pietà del core
hanno di lagrimar sofferta pena,
sì che per vinti son remasi omai.
   Ora, s'i' voglio sfogar lo dolore,
che a poco a poco a la morte mi mena,   5
convenemi parlar traendo guai.
   E perché me ricorda ch'io parlai
de la mia donna, mentre che vivia,
donne gentili, volentier con vui,
non vòi parlare altrui,   10
se non a cor gentil che in donna sia;
e dicerò di lei piangendo, pui
che si n'è gita in ciel subitamente,
e ha lasciato Amor meco dolente.

   Ita n'è Bëatrice in l'alto cielo,   15
nel reame ove li angeli hanno pace,
e sta con loro, e voi, donne, ha lassate:
   no la ci tolse qualità di gelo
né di calore, come l'altre face,
ma solo fue sua gran benignitate;   20
   ché luce de la sua umilitate
passò li cieli con tanta vertute,
che fé maravigliar l'etterno Sire,
sì che dolce disire
lo giunse di chiamar tanta salute;   25
e fella di qua giù a sé venire,
perché vedea ch'esta vita noiosa
non era degna di sì gentil cosa.

   Partissi de la sua bella persona
piena di grazia l'anima gentile,   30
ed èssi glorïosa in loco degno.

47

1. My eyes that grieve because of my heart's anguish have been so afflicted with weeping that now they are exhausted: so if now I would give vent to the grief that brings me gradually to death, I must lament in words. And remembering, gentle ladies, that while my lady was alive I was glad to speak of her with you, I will speak to none but to such gentle hearts as may be found in women; and I shall speak of her lamenting, since she has suddenly departed to heaven, leaving Love with me sorrowing.

2. Beatrice has departed to heaven on high, to the kingdom where the angels have peace; and now she is with them, having left you here, ladies. It was not the quality of cold that took her from us, nor of heat, as these things take others, but only her great goodness; for a light from her humility passed up through the heavens with such power as to cause the eternal Lord to marvel; so that a sweet desire came to Him to summon such perfection; and He made her come to Him from here below, seeing that this wretched life was not worthy of so noble a creature.

3. Full of grace the noble soul departed from the fair body, and is now in glory in the place worthy of it

Chi no la piange, quando ne ragiona,
core ha di pietra sì malvagio e vile,
ch'entrar no i puote spirito benegno.
      Non è di cor villan sì alto ingegno,   35
che possa imaginar di lei alquanto,
e però no li ven di pianger doglia:
ma ven tristizia e voglia
di sospirare e di morir di pianto,
e d'onne consolar l'anima spoglia   40
chi vede nel pensero alcuna volta
quale ella fue, e com'ella n'è tolta.

      Dannomi angoscia li sospiri forte,
quando 'l pensero ne la mente grave
mi reca quella che m'ha 'l cor diviso: 45
      e spesse fiate pensando a la morte,
venemene un disio tanto soave,
che mi tramuta lo color nel viso.
      E quando 'l maginar mi ven ben fiso,
giugnemi tanta pena d'ogne parte,   50
ch'io mi riscuoto per dolor ch'i' sento;
e sì fatto divento,
che da le genti vergogna mi parte.
Poscia piangendo, sol nel mio lamento
chiamo Beatrice, e dico: 'Or se' tu morta?'   55
e mentre ch'io la chiamo, me conforta.

      Pianger di doglia e sospirar d'angoscia
mi strugge 'l core ovunque sol mi trovo,
sì che ne 'ncrescerebbe a chi m'audesse:
      e quale è stata la mia vita, poscia   60
che la mia donna andò nel secol novo,
lingua non è che dicer lo sapesse:

Anyone who does not mourn when speaking of her has a heart of stone, so evil and base that no spirit of kindness can enter it. The mean heart lacks a mind lofty enough to form any image of her, hence no pang of mourning comes to it. But to those who from time to time see in thought what she was, and how she has been taken from us, come sorrow and a desire to sigh and to die of weeping; and they strip their souls of every consolation.

4. My sighs oppress me grievously when thought brings back to my heavy mind the death that has cleft my heart; and often, thinking of death, a desire for it comes on me, so sweet that it makes my face change colour. And when my thought is intensely fixed, then from every side such anguish comes upon me that I start up with the pain I feel; and I am brought to such a state that shame keeps me apart from everybody: and then weeping, alone, in my lament I call on Beatrice saying: 'Are you now dead?' And while I call on her, she comforts me.

5. The weeping from grief and the sighing from distress wear my heart away whenever I find myself alone; so that anyone who heard me would take pity. And what my life has been since my lady passed to the next world, there is no tongue that could tell; and so, ladies, even did

e però, donne mie, pur ch'io volesse,
non vi saprei io dir ben quel ch'io sono,
sì mi fa travagliar l'acerba vita; 65
la quale è sì 'nvilita,
che ogn'om par che mi dica: 'Io t'abbandono',
veggendo la mia labbia tramortita.
Ma qual ch'io sia la mia donna il si vede,
e io ne spero ancor da lei merzede. 70

Pietosa mia canzone, or va' piangendo;
e ritruova le donne e le donzelle
a cui le tue sorelle
erano usate di portar letizia;
e tu, che se' figliuola di tristizia, 75
vatten disconsolata a star con elle.

48 (B.XXVI)

Venite a intender li sospiri miei,
oi cor gentili, ché pietà 'l disia:
li quai disconsolati vanno via,
e s'e' non fosser, di dolor morrei;

però che gli occhi mi sarebber rei, 5
molte fïate più ch'io non vorria,
lasso, di pianger sì la donna mia,
che sfogasser lo cor, piangendo lei.

Voi udirete lor chiamar sovente
la mia donna gentil, che si n'è gita 10
al secol degno de la sua vertute;

e dispregiar talora questa vita
in persona de l'anima dolente
abbandonata de la sua salute.

I wish to, I myself could not fully describe my state, so much does this bitter life torment me—this life now become so abject that everyone who sees the deathly pallor in my face seems to say: 'I despair of you.' But whatever my state may be, my lady sees it, and I still hope for recompense from her.

Congedo. My piteous song, go now weeping and find the ladies and girls to whom your sisters used to bring gladness; and—child of sorrow that you are—go off disconsolately and stay with them.

48

Come and hear my sighs, O gentle hearts—as pity desires you should—my sighs that depart unconsoled; and were it not for them I would die of grief: for then my eyes would be in debt to me far more often than I'd wish— in debt, alas, to weep so for my lady as to bring relief to my heart, weeping for her.

You will hear them often calling on my gentle lady, who has gone off to the world that is worthy of her virtue; and hear them from time to time condemning this life, in the name of the sad soul that is forsaken by its bliss.

49 (B.XXVII)

Quantunque volte, lasso, mi rimembra
ch'io non debbo già mai
veder la donna ond'io vo sì dolente,
   tanto dolore intorno 'l cor m'assembra
la dolorosa mente,   5
ch'io dico: 'Anima mia, ché non ten vai?
   ché li tormenti che tu porterai
nel secol, che t'è già tanto noioso,
mi fan pensoso di paura forte.'
Ond'io chiamo la Morte,   10
come soave e dolce mio riposo;
e dico 'Vieni a me' con tanto amore,
che sono astioso di chiunque more.

   E' si raccoglie ne li miei sospiri
un sono di pietate,   15
che va chiamando Morte tuttavia:
   a lei si volser tutti i miei disiri,
quando la donna mia
fu giunta da la sua crudelitate;
   perché 'l piacere de la sua bieltate,   20
partendo sé da la nostra veduta,
divenne spiriтal bellezza grande,
che per lo cielo spande
luce d'amor, che li angeli saluta,
e lo intelletto loro alto, sottile   25
face maravigliar, sì v'è gentile.

50 (B.XXX)

Primo cominciamento

Era venuta ne la mente mia
la gentil donna che per suo valore
fu posta da l'altissimo signore
nel ciel de l'umiltate, ov'è Maria.

49

Alas, whenever I remember that I must never again see the lady on whose account I grieve, sorrowing memory brings such pain around my heart that I say: 'My soul, why do you not depart? For the suffering you will have to bear in this world—already so tedious to you—greatly oppresses my thoughts with fear.' So I call upon Death as my dear and sweet repose, and say: 'Come to me', with so much love that I am bitterly envious of all who die.

My sighs gather together into a pitiful sound that calls continually on Death, to whom all my desires turned once my lady was seized by his harsh power. For the loveliness of her beauty, when it withdrew from our sight, became a great spiritual beauty that now spreads a light of love through heaven, a light that gives joy to the angels and rouses wonder in their high subtle intellects, so noble is it in that place!

50

First Beginning

There had come into my heart the gentle lady who for her perfection was placed by the most high Lord in the heaven of humility where Mary is.

Era venuta ne la mente mia
quella donna gentil cui piange Amore,
entro 'n quel punto che lo suo valore
vi trasse a riguardar quel ch'eo facia.

Amor, che ne la mente la sentìa,   5
s'era svegliato nel destrutto core,
e diceva a' sospiri: 'Andate fore';
per che ciascun dolente si partìa.

Piangendo uscivan for de lo mio petto
con una voce che sovente mena   10
le lagrime dogliose a li occhi tristi.

Ma quei che n'uscian for con maggior pena,
venian dicendo: 'Oi nobile intelletto,
oggi fa l'anno che nel ciel salisti.'

51 (B. XXXI)

Videro li occhi miei quanta pietate
era apparita in la vostra figura,
quando guardaste li atti e la statura
ch'io faccio per dolor molte fïate.

Allor m'accorsi che voi pensavate   5
la qualità de la mia vita oscura,
sì che mi giunse ne lo cor paura
di dimostrar con li occhi mia viltate.

E tolsimi dinanzi a voi, sentendo
che si movean le lagrime dal core,   10
ch'era sommosso da la vostra vista.

Io dicea poscia ne l'anima trista:
'Ben è con quella donna quello Amore
lo qual mi face andar così piangendo.'

There had come into my mind that gentle lady mourned by Love, at the very moment when her perfection drew you to look at what I was doing. Love, feeling her in my mind, had awoken in my ravaged heart, and said to my sighs, 'Go forth'; so each one went off sorrowing.

Lamenting they left my breast, with a voice that often brings tears to my sad eyes. But those that issued with most pain were those that came out saying: 'O noble mind, it is a year today since you went up to heaven.'

51

My eyes saw what pity was in your face as you looked at the bearing and aspect that I often show in my grief. Then I understood that you were pondering on this sad life of mine, so that a fear seized my heart of showing my weakness through my eyes.

And I withdrew from your presence, feeling the tears welling from my heart that was stirred by the sight of you. Then in my sad soul I said: 'The same Love who makes me go thus weeping is certainly with that lady.'

52 (B.XXXII)

Color d'amore e di pietà sembianti
non preser mai così mirabilmente
viso di donna, per veder sovente
occhi gentili o dolorosi pianti,

come lo vostro, qualora davanti   5
vedetevi la mia labbia dolente;
sì che per voi mi ven cosa a la mente,
ch'io temo forte non lo cor si schianti.

Eo non posso tener li occhi distrutti
che non reguardin voi spesse fïate,   10
per desiderio di pianger ch'elli hanno:

e voi crescete sì lor volontate,
che de la voglia si consuman tutti:
ma lagrimar dinanzi a voi non sanno.

53 (B.XXXIII)

'L'amaro lagrimar che voi faceste,
oi occhi miei, così lunga stagione,
facea lagrimar l'altre persone
de la pietate, come voi vedeste.

Ora mi par che voi l'oblïereste,   5
s'io fosse dal mio lato sì fellone,
ch'i' non ven disturbasse ogne cagione,
membrandovi colei cui voi piangeste.

La vostra vanità mi fa pensare,
e spaventami sì, ch'io temo forte   10
del viso d'una donna che vi mira.

Voi non dovreste mai, se non per morte,
la vostra donna, ch'è morta, oblïare.'
Così dice 'l meo core, e poi sospira.

52

The colour of love and looks expressing pity never so marvellously took possession of a woman's face, at the repeated sight of gentle eyes and sorrowful tears, as they do of yours, whenever you see my sorrowing countenance before you; so that through you I recall something to mind, such that I fear my heart may break.

I cannot hold back my wasted eyes from looking at you time and again, in their desire to weep. And you increase this desire of theirs so much that they are all consumed by it; yet they cannot weep in your presence.

53

'O my eyes, that bitter weeping of yours, so long continued, has made others weep with pity, as you have seen. But now it seems to me you would forget that weeping, if for my part I were so disloyal as to fail to remove every cause of your so doing, by reminding you of her for whom you wept.

Your levity causes me anxiety—it terrifies me, so that I greatly fear the face of a woman who gazes at you. Except through death you should never forget your lady who is dead.' So speaks my heart; and then sighs.

54 (B.XXXIV)

Gentil pensero che parla di vui
sen vene a dimorar meco sovente,
e ragiona d'amor sì dolcemente,
che face consentir lo core in lui.

L'anima dice al cor: 'Chi è costui,   5
che vene a consolar la nostra mente,
ed è la sua vertù tanto possente,
ch'altro penser non lascia star con nui?'

Ei le risponde: 'Oi anima pensosa,
questi è uno spiritel novo d'amore,   10
che reca innanzi me li suoi desiri;

e la sua vita, e tutto 'l suo valore,
mosse de li occhi di quella pietosa
che si turbava de' nostri martiri.'

55 (B.XXXV)

Lasso, per forza di molti sospiri,
che nascon de' penser che son nel core,
li occhi son vinti, e non hanno valore
di riguardar persona che li miri.

E fatti son che paion due disiri   5
di lagrimare e di mostrar dolore,
e spesse volte piangon sì, ch'Amore
li 'ncerchia di corona di martiri.

Questi penseri, e li sospir ch'eo gitto,
diventan ne lo cor sì angosciosi,   10
ch'Amor vi tramortisce, sì lien dole;

però ch'elli hanno in lor li dolorosi
quel dolce nome di madonna scritto,
e de la morte sua molte parole.

54

A gentle thought that speaks of you comes often to dwell with me, and it talks so sweetly of love as to make the heart consent to it. The soul says to the heart: 'Who is this who comes to console our mind, and who has such strength as not to let any other thought remain with us?'

He answers her: 'O pensive soul, this is a new spirit of love that brings its desires before me; and its life and all its power came from the eyes of that compassionate lady who was disturbed by our suffering.'

55

Alas, by the violence of the many sighs born of the thoughts in my heart, my eyes are worn out and lack strength to return the gaze of any who might look at them. And they are become such that they seem two desires to shed tears and show sorrow; and often they weep so much that Love circles them with a crown of suffering.

These thoughts and the sighs I heave have become so oppressive in my heart that Love faints away there, it so grieves him; because they, the sorrowing ones, have in them that sweet name of my lady written, and many words concerning her death.

56 (B.XXXVI)

Deh peregrini che pensosi andate,
forse di cosa che non v'è presente,
venite voi da sì lontana gente,
com'a la vista voi ne dimostrate,

che non piangete quando voi passate   5
per lo suo mezzo la città dolente,
come quelle persone che nëente
par che 'ntendesser la sua gravitate?

Se voi restaste per volerlo audire,
certo lo cor de' sospiri mi dice   10
che lagrimando n'uscireste pui.

Ell'ha perduta la sua bëatrice;
e le parole ch'om di lei pò dire
hanno vertù di far piangere altrui.

57 (B.XXXVII)

Oltre la spera che più larga gira
passa 'l sospiro ch'esce del mio core:
intelligenza nova, che l'Amore
piangendo mette in lui, pur su lo tira.

Quand'elli è giunto là dove disira,   5
vede una donna, che riceve onore,
e luce sì, che per lo suo splendore
lo peregrino spirito la mira.

Vedela tal, che quando 'l mi ridice,
io no lo intendo, sì parla sottile   10
al cor dolente, che lo fa parlare.

So io che parla di quella gentile,
però che spesso ricorda Beatrice,
sì ch'io lo 'ntendo ben, donne mie care.

56

O pilgrims who go lost in thought, perhaps of some absent thing, do you come from such far-off people (as you show by your appearance) as not to weep as you pass through the midst of the sorrowing city, like those who seem to understand nothing of her affliction?

If you were to tarry from a desire to hear of it, then my sighing heart tells me that you would go hence weeping. She has lost the one who brought her joy; and even the words one can say of her have the power to make others weep.

57

Beyond the sphere that circles widest passes the sigh that issues from my heart: a new understanding which Love, lamenting, imparts to him draws him ever upwards. When he arrives where he desires to be, he sees a lady who receives honour and who shines so that the pilgrim spirit contemplates her for her splendour.

He sees her such that when he repeats this to me I do not understand, so subtly does he speak to the sorrowing heart that makes him speak. I know he speaks of that noble one, for he often mentions Beatrice; so that I understand him well, my dear ladies.

57*a* (B.XXXVIII)

CECCO ANGIOLIERI A DANTE

Dante Allaghier, Cecco, 'l tu' servo e amico,
si raccomanda a te com'a segnore:
e sì ti prego per lo dio d'amore,
lo qual è stato un tu' signor antico,

che mi perdoni s'i' spiacer ti dico,   5
ché mi dà sicurtà 'l tu' gentil core:
quel ch'i' ti dico è di questo tenore,
ch'al tu' sonetto in parte contradico.

Ch'al meo parer, ne l'una muta dice
che non intendi su' sottil parlare,   10
a que' che vide la tua Bëatrice;

e puoi hai detto a le tue donne care
che tu lo 'ntendi; e dunque contradice
a se medesmo questo tu' trovare.

58 (B.CXVII)

Per quella via che la bellezza corre
quando a svegliare Amor va ne la mente,
passa Lisetta baldanzosamente,
come colei che mi si crede tòrre.

E quando è giunta a piè di quella torre   5
che s'apre quando l'anima acconsente,
odesi voce dir subitamente:
'Volgiti, bella donna, e non ti porre:

però che dentro un'altra donna siede,
la qual di signoria chiese la verga   10
tosto che giunse, e Amor glile diede.'

57a

Dante Alighieri, your servant and friend Cecco commends himself to you as to his lord: and by the god of love—your lord from of old—I beg your pardon if I say something disagreeable—your gentle heart gives me confidence to speak. What I say comes to this, that in part I contradict your sonnet.

For it seems to me that in one tercet you say you don't understand the subtle speech of him who saw your Beatrice; after which you told your dear ladies that you understood it: therefore this poem of yours contradicts itself.

58

Along the way which beauty runs when it enters the mind to awaken Love, Lisetta goes gaily, as one who thinks she can take me. And when she reaches the foot of that tower which opens when the soul consents, suddenly a voice is heard: 'Turn away, fair lady. Do not stay: for here within reigns another lady who asked for the ruler's sceptre as soon as she arrived; and Love gave it

Quando Lisetta accommiatar si vede
da quella parte dove Amore alberga,
tutta dipinta di vergogna riede.

59 (B.LXXIX)

Voi che 'ntendendo il terzo ciel movete,
udite il ragionar ch'è nel mio core,
ch'io nol so dire altrui, sì mi par novo.

  El ciel che segue lo vostro valore,
gentili creature che voi sete,
mi tragge ne lo stato ov'io mi trovo.

  Onde 'l parlar de la vita ch'io provo,
par che si drizzi degnamente a vui:
però vi priego che lo mi 'ntendiate.
Io vi dirò del cor la novitate,
come l'anima trista piange in lui,
e come un spirto contra lei favella,
che vien pe' raggi de la vostra stella.

  Suol esser vita de lo cor dolente
un soave penser, che se ne gìa
molte fïate a' piè del nostro Sire,
  ove una donna glorïar vedia,
di cui parlava me sì dolcemente
che l'anima dicea: 'Io men vo' gire.'
  Or apparisce chi lo fa fuggire
e segnoreggia me di tal virtute,
che 'l cor ne trema che di fuori appare.
Questi mi face una donna guardare,
e dice: 'Chi veder vuol la salute,
faccia che li occhi d'esta donna miri,
sed e' non teme angoscia di sospiri.'

  Trova contraro tal che lo distrugge
l'umil pensero, che parlar mi sole
d'un'angela che 'n cielo è coronata.

her.' Lisetta, seeing herself dismissed from Love's dwelling, turns back all painted with shame.

59

1. O you who move the third heaven by intellection, listen to the speech in my heart; it is so strange, I can declare it to no others. The heaven that moves following your power, noble creatures that you are, draws me into my present state; hence it seems that speech about the life I experience should properly be addressed to you: so let me beg your attention. I will tell you of my heart's strange condition—how my sad soul weeps in it, and how a spirit disputes with her, that comes in the rays from your star.

2. The life of my sorrowing heart used to be a gentle thought which would often take its way to the feet of our Lord, where it saw a lady in glory of whom it would speak to me so sweetly that my soul would declare: 'I wish to go there too.' But now one appears who puts it to flight, and who lords it over me with such power that the trembling in my heart is made visible. This newcomer makes me look at a woman, saying: 'Let him who would see bliss gaze into this lady's eyes, provided he does not shrink from grievous sighing.'

3. The humble thought that used to speak to me of an angel crowned in heaven now meets an adversary who

L'anima piange, sì ancor len dole,   30
e dice: 'Oh lassa a me, come si fugge
questo piatoso che m'ha consolata!'
  De li occhi miei dice questa affannata:
'Qual ora fu, che tal donna li vide!
e perché non credeano a me di lei?   35
Io dicea: "Ben ne li occhi di costei
de' star colui che le mie pari ancide!"
E non mi valse ch'io ne fossi accorta
che non mirasser tal, ch'io ne son morta.'

  'Tu non se' morta, ma se' ismarrita,   40
anima nostra, che sì ti lamenti',
dice uno spiritel d'amor gentile;
  'ché quella bella donna che tu senti,
ha transmutata in tanto la tua vita,
che n'hai paura, sì se' fatta vile!   45
  Mira quant'ell'è pietosa e umile,
saggia e cortese ne la sua grandezza,
e pensa di chiamarla donna, omai!
Ché se tu non t'inganni, tu vedrai
di sì alti miracoli adornezza,   50
che tu dirai: "Amor, segnor verace,
ecco l'ancella tua; fa' che ti piace."'

  Canzone, io credo che saranno radi
color che tua ragione intendan bene,
tanto la parli faticosa e forte.   55
Onde, se per ventura elli addivene
che tu dinanzi da persone vadi
che non ti paian d'essa bene accorte,
allor ti priego che ti riconforte,
dicendo lor, diletta mia novella: 60
'Ponete mente almen com'io son bella!'

destroys it. The soul laments, still grieving at the plight of that thought, and says: 'Alas, how it flees, the compassionate one who consoled me!' And she, my troubled soul, says of my eyes: 'Unlucky moment when such a woman saw them! And why did they not believe me about her? For I said: "Truly in her eyes must dwell the one who slays such as I am." But it was no use my being alert; it did not prevent them from gazing at a woman who is such that I die of the gazing.'

4. 'You are not dead but only bewildered, you, our soul, who lament so much.' Thus speaks a gentle spirit of love. 'For that fair lady whose power you feel has so transformed your life that you are frightened—so faint-hearted have you become! See how compassionate and gentle she is, how wise and courteous in her greatness; and resolve to call her your lady henceforth. For unless you stray from the truth you will see the beauty of such high marvels as will cause you to say: "Love, true lord, behold your handmaid—do whatever you will."'

Congedo. My song, I think they will be few who clearly understand your meaning, so intricate and difficult is your speech. So then, if you happen to come before those who don't seem to see your meaning clearly, then I beg you, my new darling, take heart and say to them: 'At least consider how fair I am!'

60 (B.LXXX)

Voi che savete ragionar d'Amore,
udite la ballata mia pietosa,
che parla d'una donna disdegnosa,
la qual m'ha tolto il cor per suo valore.

    Tanto disdegna qualunque la mira,   5
che fa chinare gli occhi di paura,
    però che intorno a' suoi sempre si gira
d'ogni crudelitate una pintura;
    ma dentro portan la dolze figura
ch'a l'anima gentil fa dir: 'Merzede!',   10
sì vertüosa, che quando si vede,
trae li sospiri altrui fora del core.

    Par ch'ella dica: 'Io non sarò umile
verso d'alcun che ne li occhi mi guardi,
    ch'io ci porto entro quel segnor gentile   15
che m'ha fatto sentir de li suoi dardi.'
    E certo i' credo che così li guardi
per vederli per sé quando le piace,
a quella guisa retta donna face
quando si mira per volere onore.   20

    Io non ispero che mai per pietate
degnasse di guardare un poco altrui,
    così è fera donna in sua bieltate
questa che sente Amor ne gli occhi sui.
    Ma quanto vuol nasconda e guardi lui,   25
ch'io non veggia talor tanta salute;
però che i miei disiri avran vertute
contra 'l disdegno che mi dà tremore.

60

O you who know how to reason about Love, listen to my pitiful ballata, that speaks of a disdainful lady whose power has robbed me of my heart.

1. She so disdains any who look at her, it makes them lower their eyes in fear; for her eyes are always encircled by an image of all harshness. And yet within them they bear the lovely form that makes the noble soul say, 'have pity!'—a form of such power that, once seen, it draws sighs from one's heart.

2. She seems to say: 'I shall not be gentle to anyone who looks into my eyes; for therein I bear that noble Lord who has caused me to feel his shafts.' And I firmly believe that she thus withholds her eyes in order to look into them herself, as a virtuous woman does when she gazes at herself out of desire for honour.

3. I have no hope that pity will ever make her deign to turn her gaze a little upon others, so harsh in her beauty is this lady who feels Love in her eyes. But let her hide and withhold him as much as she will, to prevent me from ever glimpsing such beatitude; my desires will none the less prevail against the scorn that makes me tremble.

61 (B.LXXXI)

Amor che ne la mente mi ragiona
de la mia donna disïosamente,
move cose di lei meco sovente,
che lo 'ntelletto sovr'esse disvia.
    Lo suo parlar sì dolcemente sona,   5
che l'anima ch'ascolta e che lo sente
dice: 'Oh me lassa, ch'io non son possente
di dir quel ch'odo de la donna mia!'
    E certo e' mi conven lasciare in pria,
s'io vo' trattar di quel ch'odo di lei,   10
ciò che lo mio intelletto non comprende;
e di quel che s'intende
gran parte, perché dirlo non savrei.
Però, se le mie rime avran difetto
ch'entreran ne la loda di costei,   15
di ciò si biasmi il debole intelletto
e 'l parlar nostro, che non ha valore
di ritrar tutto ciò che dice Amore.

    Non vede il sol, che tutto 'l mondo gira,
cosa tanto gentil, quanto in quell'ora   20
che luce ne la parte ove dimora
la donna, di cui dire Amor mi face.
    Ogni Intelletto di là su la mira,
e quella gente che qui s'innamora
ne' lor pensieri la truovano ancora,   25
quando Amor fa sentir de la sua pace.
    Suo esser tanto a Quei che lel dà piace,
che 'nfonde sempre in lei la sua vertute
oltre 'l dimando di nostra natura.
La sua anima pura,   30
che riceve da lui questa salute,
lo manifesta in quel ch'ella conduce:

61

1. Love, speaking fervently in my mind of my lady, often utters such things concerning her that my intellect is bewildered by them. His speech sounds so sweetly that the soul, as she attends and hears, says: 'Alas that I am unable to express what I hear of my lady!' And certainly, if I wish to treat of what I hear of her, I must first leave aside what my intellect does not grasp; and then, too, much of what it does understand, for I should not be able to express it. If then these words of mine which undertake her praise be found wanting, let the blame fall on the weak intellect, and on our faculty of speech which lacks the power to record all that Love says.

2. The sun that circles the whole world never sees anything so noble as when its light falls there where dwells the lady of whom Love makes me speak. All Intelligences on high gaze at her, and those who here below are in love still find her in their thoughts, when Love brings them to partake of his peace. So much does her being please Him who gives it her that He continually pours His power into her beyond the requirement of our nature. Her pure soul makes it clear through what she governs that she receives this perfection from Him;

ché 'n sue bellezze son cose vedute
che li occhi di color dov'ella luce
ne mandan messi al cor pien di desiri,   35
che prendon aire e diventan sospiri.

In lei discende la virtù divina
sì come face in angelo che 'l vede;
e qual donna gentil questo non crede,
vada con lei e miri li atti sui.   40
Quivi dov'ella parla, si dichina
un spirito da ciel, che reca fede
come l'alto valor ch'ella possiede
è oltre quel che si conviene a nui.
Li atti soavi ch'ella mostra altrui   45
vanno chiamando Amor ciascuno a prova
in quella voce che lo fa sentire.
Di costei si può dire:
gentile è in donna ciò che in lei si trova,
e bello è tanto quanto lei simiglia.   50
E puossi dir che 'l suo aspetto giova
a consentir ciò che par maraviglia;
onde la nostra fede è aiutata:
però fu tal da etterno ordinata.

Cose appariscon ne lo suo aspetto   55
che mostran de' piacer di Paradiso,
dico ne li occhi e nel suo dolce riso,
che le vi reca Amor com'a suo loco.
Elle soverchian lo nostro intelletto,
come raggio di sole un frale viso: 60
e perch'io non le posso mirar fiso,
mi conven contentar di dirne poco.

for among her beauties such things are seen that the eyes of those on whom her light falls send to the heart messengers full of longing, which gather air and turn into sighs.

3. The divine goodness descends into her in the same way as into an angel that sees Him; and let any noble lady who does not believe this keep her company and contemplate her bearing. Whenever she speaks a spirit comes down from heaven to testify that the high perfection she possesses transcends our measure. The gracious actions that she displays vie with each other in calling on Love with such a voice as must awaken him. Of her it can be said: nobility in woman is what is found in her, and beauty is all that resembles her. Further, it can be said that her aspect helps to induce belief in what seems miraculous; and so our faith is strengthened: and it was for this that she was established from eternity.

4. In her aspect things appear that show the joys of Paradise—I mean in her eyes and her lovely smile; for it is there, as to the place which belongs to him, that Love leads them. And they overpower our intellect as a ray of sunlight overpowers a weak sight; and since I cannot look steadily at them I must be content to write but little of them. Her beauty showers down flames of

Sua bieltà piove fiammelle di foco,
animate d'un spirito gentile
ch'è creatore d'ogni pensier bono;   65
e rompon come trono
l'innati vizii che fanno altrui vile.
Però qual donna sente sua bieltate
biasmar per non parer queta e umile,
miri costei ch'è essemplo d'umiltate!   70
Questa è colei ch'umilia ogni perverso:
costei pensò chi mosse l'universo.

Canzone, e' par che tu parli contraro
al dir d'una sorella che tu hai;
ché questa donna, che tanto umil fai,   75
ella la chiama fera e disdegnosa.
Tu sai che 'l ciel sempr'è lucente e chiaro,
e quanto in sé non si turba già mai;
ma li nostri occhi per cagioni assai
chiaman la stella talor tenebrosa.   80
Così, quand'ella la chiama orgogliosa,
non considera lei secondo il vero,
ma pur secondo quel ch'a lei parea:
ché l'anima temea,
e teme ancora, sì che mi par fero   85
quantunqu'io veggio là 'v'ella mi senta.
Così ti scusa, se ti fa mestero;
e quando pòi, a lei ti rappresenta:
dirai: 'Madonna, s'ello v'è a grato,
io parlerò di voi in ciascun lato.'   90

fire alive with a lofty spirit, the creator of all good thoughts; and like a lightning flash they shatter the inborn vices that debase one. Therefore let every woman who hears her beauty slighted for seeming to lack gentleness and humility, gaze at this lady, the very model of humility! She it is who brings back to humility whoever strays from it. She was in the mind of Him who set the universe in motion.

Congedo. My song, it seems you speak in a sense contrary to one of your sisters, seeing that this lady, whom you declare so humble, she calls harsh and scornful. You know that the sky is always shining and clear and never itself grows dark; and yet our eyes, for a number of reasons, sometimes say the stars are dimmed. Similarly, when your sister calls this lady 'proud', she does not consider her as she really is, but only as the lady seemed to her. For my soul was afraid, and indeed it is still afraid, so that whatever I see, when this lady perceives me, seems harsh. Make your excuses thus, should the need arise; and when you can, present yourself to her and say: 'Lady, if it be your wish, I will speak of you everywhere.'

62 (B.LXXXIV)

Parole mie che per lo mondo siete,
voi che nasceste poi ch'io cominciai
a dir per quella donna in cui errai:
'Voi che 'ntendendo il terzo ciel movete',

andatevene a lei, che la sapete,   5
chiamando sì ch'ell'oda i vostri guai;
ditele: 'Noi siam vostre, ed unquemai
più che noi siamo non ci vederete.'

Con lei non state, ché non v'è Amore;
ma gite a torno in abito dolente   10
a guisa de le vostre antiche sore.

Quando trovate donna di valore,
gittatelevi a' piedi umilemente,
dicendo: 'A voi dovem noi fare onore.'

63 (B.LXXXV)

O dolci rime che parlando andate
de la donna gentil che l'altre onora,
a voi verrà, se non è giunto ancora,
un che direte: 'Questi è nostro frate.'

Io vi scongiuro che non l'ascoltiate,   5
per quel signor che le donne innamora,
ché ne la sua sentenzia non dimora
cosa che amica sia di veritate.

E se voi foste per le sue parole
mosse a venire inver la donna vostra,   10
non v'arrestate, ma venite a lei.

Dite: 'Madonna, la venuta nostra
è per raccomandarvi un che si dole,
dicendo: "Ov'è 'l disio de li occhi miei?"'

62

Words of mine that have gone about the world, you that were born when I began to write for that lady in whom I was deceived, *Voi che 'ntendendo il terzo ciel movete*; go now to this lady whom you know, and call on her so that she listens to your laments, saying: 'We belong to you, but you will never see any others apart from ourselves.'

Do not stay with her, for Love is not there, but go around in clothes that show grief, like your elder sisters. When you meet a woman worthy of love, throw yourselves humbly at her feet and say: 'It is you whom we must honour.'

63

O you sweet poems that go about speaking of that noble lady who brings honour to others, one is about to join you (if he has not done so already) of whom you will say: 'He is our brother.' I adjure you, by that Lord who makes ladies love, do not listen to him, for there is nothing friendly to truth in what he says.

But if because of his words you have set out to approach your lady, do not stop, but go to her and say: 'Lady, the purpose of our coming is to commend to you one who is sad and who says, "Where is the desire of my eyes?"'

64 (B.LXXXVII)

'I' mi son pargoletta bella e nova,
che son venuta per mostrare altrui
de le bellezze del loco ond'io fui.

   I' fui del cielo, e tornerovvi ancora
per dar de la mia luce altrui diletto;   5
   e chi mi vede e non se ne innamora
d'amor non averà mai intelletto,
   ché non mi fu in piacer alcun disdetto
quando natura mi chiese a Colui
che volle, donne, accompagnarmi a vui.   10

   Ciascuna stella ne li occhi mi piove
del lume suo e de la sua vertute;
   le mie bellezze sono al mondo nove,
però che di là su mi son venute:
   le quai non posson esser canosciute   15
se non da canoscenza d'omo in cui
Amor si metta per piacer altrui.'

   Queste parole si leggon nel viso
d'un'angioletta che ci è apparita:
   e io che per veder lei mirai fiso,   20
ne sono a rischio di perder la vita;
   però ch'io ricevetti tal ferita
da un ch'io vidi dentro a li occhi sui,
ch'i' vo piangendo e non m'acchetai pui.

65 (B.LXXXVIII)

Perché ti vedi giovinetta e bella,
tanto che svegli ne la mente Amore,
pres'hai orgoglio e durezza nel core.

64

'I am a young girl, lovely and marvellous, who has come to show men something of the beauty of the place whence I came.

1. I came from heaven and shall return there once more, to delight others with my light; and anyone who sees me and does not fall in love with me will never have understanding of love; for nothing that makes for beauty was denied me when Nature begged me of Him who chose to make me, ladies, your companion.

2. Every star showers its light and power into my eyes. My beauties are a marvel in this world because they came to me from on high; nor can they be known save by the knowledge of one in whom Love comes to dwell through another's beauty.'

3. These words can be read in the face of an angel who has appeared here: and I, who gazed intensely that I might see her, am in danger of losing my life thereby; for I received such a wound from one whom I saw in her eyes that now I am sorrowful, and from that moment I have had no peace.

65

Because you see you're so young and fair that you awake Love in the mind, your heart has become proud and hard.

Orgogliosa se' fatta e per me dura,
po' che d'ancider me, lasso, ti prove: 5
    credo che 'l facci per esser sicura
se la vertù d'Amore a morte move.
    Ma perché preso più ch'altro mi trove,
non hai respetto alcun del mi' dolore.
Possi tu spermentar lo suo valore!   10

66 (B.LXXXIX)

Chi guarderà già mai sanza paura
ne li occhi d'esta bella pargoletta,
che m'hanno concio sì, che non s'aspetta
per me se non la morte, che m'è dura?

Vedete quanto è forte mia ventura: 5
ché fu tra l'altre la mia vita eletta
per dare essemplo altrui, ch'uom non si metta
in rischio di mirar la sua figura.

Destinata mi fu questa finita,
da ch'un uom convenia esser disfatto,   10
perch'altri fosse di pericol tratto;

e però, lasso, fu' io così ratto
in trarre a me 'l contrario de la vita,
come vertù di stella margherita.

67 (B.XC)

Amor, che movi tua vertù da cielo
come 'l sol lo splendore,
che là s'apprende più lo suo valore
dove più nobiltà suo raggio trova;

Proud you have become and hard towards me, since, alas, you seek to kill me; and this I think you do in order to discover whether the power of Love leads to death. But finding me held captive more than any other, you have no thought at all for my suffering. May you too experience his power!

66

Who will ever look without fear into the eyes of this lovely girl, the eyes which have reduced me to such a state that now I expect only death, a bitter death? See how hard is my plight—for my life was chosen from all others to serve as an example to men not to dare take the risk of gazing at her face.

Such an end was my destiny, since one man had to be destroyed that others might be saved from danger; and this, alas, is why I was as prompt in drawing to myself life's contrary as a pearl is to draw in the influence of a star.

67

1. Love, who send down your power from heaven as the sun does its splendour—for the greater the perfection of what its beams encounter, the more its influence takes

e come el fuga oscuritate e gelo,   5
così, alto segnore,
tu cacci la viltate altrui del core,
né ira contra te fa lunga prova:
   da te conven che ciascun ben si mova
per lo qual si travaglia il mondo tutto;   10
sanza te è distrutto
quanto avemo in potenzia di ben fare,
come pintura in tenebrosa parte,
che non si può mostrare
né dar diletto di color né d'arte.   15

   Feremi ne lo cor sempre tua luce,
come raggio in la stella,
poi che l'anima mia fu fatta ancella
de la tua podestà primeramente;
   onde ha vita un disio che mi conduce   20
con sua dolce favella
in rimirar ciascuna cosa bella
con più diletto quanto è più piacente.
   Per questo mio guardar m'è ne la mente
una giovane entrata, che m'ha preso,   25
e hagli un foco acceso,
com'acqua per chiarezza fiamma accende;
perché nel suo venir li raggi tuoi,
con li quai mi risplende,
saliron tutti su ne gli occhi suoi.   30

   Quanto è ne l'esser suo bella, e gentile
ne gli atti ed amorosa,
tanto lo imaginar, che non si posa,
l'adorna ne la mente ov'io la porto:
   non che da se medesmo sia sottile   35
a così alta cosa,
ma da la tua vertute ha quel ch'elli osa
oltre al poder che natura ci ha porto.

effect: and just as it dispels darkness and cold, so do you, mighty Lord, drive baseness from the heart, nor can ill-humour resist you for long—it is from you, Love, that every good must proceed for which the whole world strives; without you all the good we might do is defeated —like a picture in a dark place unable to show itself and give delight with colour and artistry.

2. Your light has struck ceaselessly into my heart, as sunbeams strike the stars, since first my soul became servant to your power. And this gives life to a desire that leads me on with its gentle speech to gaze at all beautiful things, and with greater delight the more beautiful they are. And through this gazing a young woman has entered my mind and taken me captive; she has lit a fire there, just as water, through its clarity, kindles flame; because at her coming your beams, which she reflects on to me, all leaped back up to her eyes.

3. Beautiful as she is in her being and noble in her bearing and worthy of love, so and not less does my restless imagination adorn her in the mind where I bear her; not that of itself it has the sensitivity to apprehend so sublime an object, but from your power it receives what it is now enabled to do beyond the capacity that Nature gives us. Her beauty is a proof of your nobility

È sua beltà del tuo valor conforto,
in quanto giudicar si puote effetto   40
sovra degno suggetto,
in guisa ched è 'l sol segno di foco;
lo qual a lui non dà né to' virtute,
ma fallo in altro loco
ne l'effetto parer di più salute.   45

Dunque, segnor di sì gentil natura
che questa nobiltate
che avven qua giuso e tutt'altra bontate
lieva principio de la tua altezza,
    guarda la vita mia quanto ella è dura,   50
e prendine pietate,
ché lo tuo ardor per la costei bieltate
mi fa nel core aver troppa gravezza.
    Falle sentire, Amor, per tua dolcezza,
il gran disio ch'i' ho di veder lei;   55
non soffrir che costei
per giovanezza mi conduca a morte:
ché non s'accorge ancor com'ella piace,
né quant'io l'amo forte,
né che ne li occhi porta la mia pace.   60

Onor ti sarà grande se m'aiuti,
e a me ricco dono,
tanto quanto conosco ben ch'io sono
là 'v'io non posso difender mia vita:
    ché gli spiriti miei son combattuti   65
da tal, ch'io non ragiono,
se per tua volontà non han perdono,
che possan guari star sanza finita.

inasmuch as one can form a judgement about an effect when it is realized in matter disposed to receive it. In the same way, the sun is the term to which fire refers; for fire neither gives power to nor removes it from the sun, but, operating in a different place, it makes the sun's beneficence the more apparent in this its effect.

4. So then, O Lord, whose nature is so noble that whatever nobility is realized here below and every other form of goodness draw their origin from your majesty, consider how hard is my life and take pity on it; for your fervour that comes to me through her beauty brings unbearable suffering into my heart. Make her feel with your sweetness, Love, the great longing I have to see her. Do not permit her to bring me to death by her youth; for she is not yet aware how fair she is, nor how intensely I love her, nor that in her eyes she bears my peace.

5. If you help me, you will receive much honour and I a precious gift—since well I know that I have come to a point where I can no longer defend my life; for my spirits are assailed by a woman who is such that, unless it be your will that they should be spared, I do not think they can long survive. And further, your power will be

Ed ancor tua potenzia fia sentita
da questa bella donna, che n'è degna: 70
ché par che si convegna
di darle d'ogni ben gran compagnia,
com'a colei che fu nel mondo nata
per aver segnoria
sovra la mente d'ogni uom che la guata.   75

68 (B.XCI)

Io sento sì d'Amor la gran possanza,
ch'io non posso durare
lungamente a soffrire, ond'io mi doglio:
  però che 'l suo valor si pur avanza,
e 'l mio sento mancare   5
sì ch'io son meno ognora ch'io non soglio.
  Non dico ch'Amor faccia più ch'io voglio,
ché, se facesse quanto il voler chiede,
quella vertù che natura mi diede
nol sosterria, però ch'ella è finita: 10
ma questo è quello ond'io prendo cordoglio,
che a la voglia il poder non terrà fede;
e se di buon voler nasce merzede,
io l'addimando per aver più vita
da li occhi che nel lor bello splendore   15
portan conforto ovunque io sento amore.

  Entrano i raggi di questi occhi belli
ne' miei innamorati,
e portan dolce ovunque io sento amaro;
  e sanno lo cammin, sì come quelli   20
che già vi son passati,
e sanno il loco dove Amor lasciaro,

felt by this fair woman who is worthy of it; for clearly it is fitting to bestow on her a great retinue of all good things, born as she was into the world to hold sway over the mind of all who contemplate her.

68

1. So much do I feel Love's mighty power that to my grief I cannot bear it for long: for while his strength continually increases I feel that my own is failing—at each moment I am weaker than I was. I am not saying that Love does more than I want him to, for if he were to do what my will demands, the strength that I have from Nature, being finite, would not sustain it. In fact it is just this which grieves me, that my strength is a traitor to my desire. But if reward is born of good will, I now ask for that reward—so that I may draw more life from those eyes which with their beautiful radiance bring me consolation whenever I feel love.

2. The rays from these fair eyes enter my own loving eyes, bringing me sweetness whenever I feel bitterness. They know the way, having passed by it before, and they know the place where they left Love when, through my

quando per li occhi miei dentro il menaro:
per che merzé, volgendosi, a me fanno,
e di colei cui son procaccian danno   25
celandosi da me, poi tanto l'amo
che sol per lei servir mi tegno caro.
E' miei pensier, che pur d'amor si fanno,
come a lor segno, al suo servigio vanno:
per che l'adoperar sì forte bramo,   30
che, s'io 'l credesse far fuggendo lei,
lieve saria; ma so ch'io ne morrei.

    Ben è verace amor quel che m'ha preso,
e ben mi stringe forte,
quand'io farei quel ch'io dico per lui: 35
    ché nullo amore è di cotanto peso,
quanto è quel che la morte
face piacer, per ben servire altrui.
    E io 'n cotal voler fermato fui
sì tosto come il gran disio ch'io sento   40
fu nato per vertù del piacimento
che nel bel viso d'ogni bel s'accoglie.
Io son servente, e quando penso a cui,
qual ch'ella sia, di tutto son contento:
ché l'uom può ben servir contra talento;   45
e se merzé giovanezza mi toglie,
io spero tempo che più ragion prenda,
pur che la vita tanto si difenda.

    Quand'io penso un gentil disio, ch'è nato
del gran disio ch'io porto,   50
ch'a ben far tira tutto il mio podere,
    parmi esser di merzede oltrapagato;
e anche più, ch'a torto
mi par di servidor nome tenere:

eyes, they brought him within me. Hence, when they turn towards me they give me my reward, but when they conceal themselves they bring loss to her whose they are, since I love her so much that I value myself only in order to serve her. My thoughts, born only of love, move to her service as to their goal: for which reason my desire for action is so intense, that if I thought I could serve her by leaving her I would willingly do so; but I know that then I should die.

3. Without doubt it is true love that has taken hold of me, and strongly indeed it grips me, seeing that I would do what I say on account of it: for no love is so great as that which makes death desirable in loyal service of another. And I have been fixed in this love from the moment when the great desire I feel was born by virtue of the beauty which gathers all beauty into her beautiful face. A servant I am, and when I consider whose servant, then, no matter what her disposition, I am wholly content: for one may indeed serve against one's lady's will; and if, being young, she withholds her favour from me, I wait for the time when she'll have grown wiser—provided that my life holds out so long.

4. When I consider a noble longing—sprung from that great longing within me—which draws all my powers to good actions, it seems to me that I have recompense beyond my deserts—more, that I am misnamed a servant,

così dinanzi a li occhi del piacere   55
si fa 'l servir merzé d'altrui bontate.
Ma poi ch'io mi ristringo a veritate,
convien che tal disio servigio conti:
però che, s'io procaccio di valere,
non penso tanto a mia proprïetate   60
quanto a colei che m'ha in sua podestate,
ché 'l fo perché sua cosa in pregio monti;
e io son tutto suo: così mi tegno,
ch'Amor di tanto onor m'ha fatto degno.

Altri ch'Amor non mi potea far tale   65
ch'eo fosse degnamente
cosa di quella che non s'innamora,
   ma stassi come donna a cui non cale
de l'amorosa mente
che sanza lei non può passare un'ora.   70
   Io non la vidi tante volte ancora
ch'io non trovasse in lei nova bellezza;
onde Amor cresce in me la sua grandezza
tanto quanto il piacer novo s'aggiugne.
Ond'elli avven che tanto fo dimora   75
in uno stato, e tanto Amor m'avvezza
con un martiro e con una dolcezza,
quanto è quel tempo che spesso mi pugne,
che dura da ch'io perdo la sua vista
in fino al tempo ch'ella si racquista.   80

Canzon mia bella, se tu mi somigli,
tu non sarai sdegnosa
tanto quanto a la tua bontà s'avvene:
   però ti prego che tu t'assottigli,
dolce mia amorosa,   85
in prender modo e via che ti stea bene.

so much does service itself become a reward from another's generosity in the presence of those fair eyes. Yet since I am holding to the truth, I must reckon this desire as service, because even though I strive to be worthy I think less of myself than of her who has me in her power—my striving being for the greater glory of all that is hers. And hers I am entirely: so I regard myself, for Love has made me worthy of such honour.

5. Only Love could have made me worthily belong to one who herself does not love, but remains like a woman indifferent to the loving mind which cannot pass an hour without her. Often as I have seen her I still find in her new beauties; hence Love increases his power in me in proportion as her loveliness grows; and so it comes about that I stay in one state, and Love accustoms me to one degree of suffering and joy, just as long as that time which often torments me, that lasts from the moment I lose sight of her to when I regain it.

Congedo (1). My beautiful song, if you resemble me you will be less proud than your goodness gives you the right to be: take care, my sweet love-song, to choose a way and go in a manner becoming to you. Should a

Se cavalier t'invita o ti ritene,
imprima che nel suo piacer ti metta,
espia, se far lo puoi, de la sua setta,
se vuoi saver qual è la sua persona: 90
ché 'l buon col buon sempre camera tene.
Ma elli avven che spesso altri si getta
in compagnia che non è che disdetta
di mala fama ch'altri di lui suona:
con rei non star né a cerchio né ad arte,   95
ché non fu mai saver tener lor parte.

Canzone, a' tre men rei di nostra terra
te n'anderai prima che vadi altrove:
li due saluta, e 'l terzo vo' che prove
di trarlo fuor di mala setta in pria.   100
Digli che 'l buon col buon non prende guerra,
prima che co' malvagi vincer prove;
digli ch'è folle chi non si rimove
per tema di vergogna da follia;
ché que' la teme c'ha del mal paura,   105
per che, fuggendo l'un, l'altro assicura.

69 (B.LXXXII)

Le dolci rime d'amor ch'i solia
cercar ne' miei pensieri,
convien ch'io lasci; non perch'io non speri
ad esse ritornare,
    ma perché li atti disdegnosi e feri,   5
che ne la donna mia
sono appariti, m'han chiusa la via
de l'usato parlare.

gentleman ask you in or stop you on your way, before entrusting yourself to him, find out if you can who his friends are—if you want to know the sort of person he is: for the good always keep together (although it often happens that someone intrudes into company that simply gives the lie to the bad name commonly given him). Do not associate with the vicious for business or pleasure; it has never been wise to make common cause with them.

Congedo (2). My song, before you go anywhere else, go to the three least vicious in our city. Greet two of them; but as for the third, I want you first to try to draw him away from bad company. Tell him that a good man never quarrels with the good until he has tried to overcome those who are bad. Tell him that only a fool, fearing dishonour, will refuse to abandon his folly: for to fear dishonour is to fear evil; and thus by avoiding the one, one is safe from the other.

69

1. The sweet love-poetry I was accustomed to seek out in my thoughts I must now forsake; not that I do not hope to return to it, but the proud hard bearing that has become apparent in my lady has barred the path of my

E poi che tempo mi par d'aspettare,
diporrò giù lo mio soave stile,
ch'i' ho tenuto nel trattar d'amore;
e dirò del valore,
per lo qual veramente omo è gentile,
con rima aspr'e sottile;
riprovando 'l giudicio falso e vile
di quei che voglion che di gentilezza
sia principio ricchezza.
E, cominciando, chiamo quel signore
ch'a la mia donna ne li occhi dimora,
per ch'ella di se stessa s'innamora.

Tale imperò che gentilezza volse,
secondo 'l suo parere,
che fosse antica possession d'avere
con reggimenti belli;
   e altri fu di più lieve savere,
che tal detto rivolse,
e l'ultima particula ne tolse,
ché non l'avea fors'elli!
   Di retro da costui van tutti quelli
che fan gentile per ischiatta altrui
che lungiamente in gran ricchezza è stata;
ed è tanto durata
la così falsa oppinion tra nui,
che l'uom chiama colui
omo gentil che può dicere: 'Io fui
nepote, o figlio, di cotal valente',
benché sia da nïente.
Ma vilissimo sembra, a chi 'l ver guata,
cui è scorto 'l cammino e poscia l'erra,
e tocca a tal, ch'è morto e va per terra!

usual speech. And so, since it now seems a time for wait-
ing, I will lay down that sweet style of mine which I held
to in writing of love, and I will speak instead in harsh
and subtle rhymes concerning the quality by which man
is truly noble; refuting the false and base opinion of
those who hold that nobility depends on wealth. And
at the outset I invoke that Lord who dwells in my lady's
eyes, and thus makes her in love with herself.

2. There was a ruler of the Empire who maintained
that in his view nobility consisted in long-standing
possession of wealth together with pleasing manners; and
someone else, of shallower wit, reconsidering this dictum,
dispensed with the last little detail—lacking it perhaps
himself! In his wake follow all those who count a man
as noble for belonging to a family which has been very
rich for a long time; and so ingrained has this absurd
opinion become among us, that people call a man noble
who can say: 'I am grandson, or son, of such and such
a great man', while in himself he's a nonentity. But to
those who look at the truth, a man seems doubly base,
who, having been shown the right path, then goes astray
—so far astray that he's a dead man walking!

Chi diffinisce: 'Omo è legno animato',
prima dice non vero,
e, dopo 'l falso, parla non intero;
ma più forse non vede.
Similemente fu chi tenne impero   45
in diffinire errato,
ché prima puose 'l falso e, d'altro lato,
con difetto procede:
ché le divizie, sì come si crede,
non posson gentilezza dar né tòrre,   50
però che vili son da lor natura:
poi chi pinge figura,
se non può esser lei, non la può porre,
né la diritta torre
fa piegar rivo che da lungi corre.   55
Che siano vili appare ed imperfette,
ché, quantunque collette,
non posson quïetar, ma dan più cura;
onde l'animo ch'è dritto e verace
per lor discorrimento non si sface.   60

Né voglion che vil uom gentil divegna,
né di vil padre scenda
nazion che per gentil già mai s'intenda;
questo è da lor confesso:
onde lor ragion par che sé offenda   65
in tanto quanto assegna
che tempo a gentilezza si convegna,
diffinendo con esso.

3. If anyone says: 'Man is an animate tree': first what he says isn't true, and then, after the falsehood, he is leaving the definition incomplete—but perhaps he can see no further. Mistaken in just this way was he who ruled the Empire: for, first he has stated a falsehood and then, this apart, what he goes on to say is deficient. For—contrary to what is generally believed—riches cannot either confer or take away nobility, being themselves base by nature: thus he who paints a form, if he cannot 'be' it, cannot set it down; nor is an upright tower made to lean by a stream that flows at a distance. That riches are base and defective is clear from this, that in whatever quantity they are amassed, they bring no peace but only increasing anxiety: hence the mind that is upright and truthful is not shattered by their loss.

4. Now my opponents maintain that a base man can never himself become noble, and that the offspring of a base father can never be reckoned noble: this is what they say. Clearly then their position is self-contradictory, inasmuch as they make time a factor in nobility, including it in their definition. Again, it follows from the

Ancor, segue di ciò che innanzi ho messo,
che siam tutti gentili o ver villani,   70
o che non fosse ad uom cominciamento:
ma ciò io non consento,
ned ellino altressì, se son cristiani!
Per che a 'ntelletti sani
è manifesto i lor diri esser vani,   75
e io così per falsi li riprovo,
e da lor mi rimovo;
e dicer voglio omai, sì com'io sento,
che cosa è gentilezza, e da che vene,
e dirò i segni che 'l gentile uom tene.   80

Dico ch'ogni vertù principalmente
vien da una radice:
vertute, dico, che fa l'uom felice
in sua operazione.
Questo è, secondo che l'Etica dice,   85
un abito eligente
lo qual dimora in mezzo solamente,
e tai parole pone.
Dico che nobiltate in sua ragione
importa sempre ben del suo subietto,   90
come viltate importa sempre male;
e vertute cotale
dà sempre altrui di sé buono intelletto;
per che in medesmo detto
convegnono ambedue, ch'en d'uno effetto.   95
Onde convien da l'altra vegna l'una,
o d'un terzo ciascuna;
ma se l'una val ciò che l'altra vale,
e ancor più, da lei verrà più tosto.
E ciò ch'io dett'ho qui sia per supposto.   100

foregoing that either we are all noble or all plebeian, or else that mankind didn't have one beginning; but this alternative I do not admit, and neither do they if they are Christians. Consequently it is clear to every healthy mind that their statements are groundless; and so, having refuted them as false, I turn away from them. And now I for my part will say what I think about nobility—what it is, whence it comes, and the distinctive features that a noble person possesses.

5. I affirm that every virtue stems ultimately from one root, meaning by virtue that which makes a man happy in his actions. This is, as the Ethics states, a 'habit of choosing which keeps steadily to the mean'—those are the very words. And I say that nobility by definition always connotes a good in him who has it, as baseness always connotes something bad. Similarly virtue, as defined above, is always understood as good. Hence, since both have the same effect, both concur in one definition. Hence it must be that either one is derived from the other, or each from a third thing. But if one comprehends the other and something else as well, then this is the one more likely to be the origin. And let all this be presupposed in what follows.

È gentilezza dovunqu'è vertute,
ma non vertute ov'ella;
sì com'è 'l cielo dovunqu'è la stella,
ma ciò non *e converso*.
    E noi in donna e in età novella   105
vedem questa salute,
in quanto vergognose son tenute,
ch'è da vertù diverso.
    Dunque verrà, come dal nero il perso,
ciascheduna vertute da costei,   110
o vero il gener lor, ch'io misi avanti.
Però nessun si vanti
dicendo: 'Per ischiatta io son con lei',
ch'elli son quasi dei
quei c'han tal grazia fuor di tutti rei: 115
ché solo Iddio a l'anima la dona
che vede in sua persona
perfettamente star: sì ch'ad alquanti
che seme di felicità sia costa,
messo da Dio ne l'anima ben posta.   120

    L'anima cui adorna esta bontate
non la si tiene ascosa,
ché dal principio ch'al corpo si sposa
la mostra infin la morte.
    Ubidente, soave e vergognosa   125
è ne la prima etate,
e sua persona adorna di bieltate
con le sue parti accorte;

6. Nobility is wherever virtue is, but virtue is not wherever nobility is; just as the sky is wherever a star is, but not *e converso*. And we see this goodness in women and in the young, in so far as they are held to be shy and bashful, which is something distinct from virtue. Hence each virtue—or rather the above-mentioned common factor in virtue—derives from nobility as perse from black. And therefore let no one boast saying: 'I am noble because of my birth'; for those who have this grace without any flaw are almost godlike; for it is God alone who gives it to a soul which He sees to be in perfect harmony with her body. Hence it is clear to some that nobility is the seed of happiness placed by God in a well-disposed soul.

7. The soul whom this goodness adorns does not keep it concealed; for from the beginning, from the moment she weds with the body, she displays it even until death. In her first age she is obedient, sweet, and bashful, and she adorns her body with the beauty of well-matched

in giovinezza, temperata e forte,
piena d'amore e di cortese lode, 130
e solo in lealtà far si diletta;
è ne la sua senetta
prudente e giusta, e larghezza se n'ode,
e 'n se medesma gode
d'udire e ragionar de l'altrui prode; 135
poi ne la quarta parte de la vita
a Dio si rimarita,
contemplando la fine che l'aspetta,
e benedice li tempi passati.
Vedete omai quanti son l'ingannati! 140

    Contra-li-erranti mia, tu te n'andrai;
e quando tu sarai
in parte dove sia la donna nostra,
non le tenere il tuo mestier coverto:
tu le puoi dir per certo: 145
'Io vo parlando de l'amica vostra.'

70 (B.LXXXIII)

Poscia ch'Amor del tutto m'ha lasciato,
non per mio grato,
ché stato   non avea tanto gioioso,
ma però che pietoso
fu tanto del meo core, 5
che non sofferse d'ascoltar suo pianto;
    i' canterò così disamorato
contra 'l peccato,
ch'è nato   in noi, di chiamare a ritroso
tal ch'è vile e noioso 10
con nome di valore,
cioè di leggiadria, ch'è bella tanto

parts. In the prime of life she is self-controlled and strong, full of love and wins great praise for courtesy, and she takes delight only in observing the law. In old age she is prudent and just, and has a reputation for generosity, and rejoices to hear and speak well of others. Finally, in the fourth phase of life she returns to God as a bride, contemplating the end that awaits her and blessing the stages through which she has passed. See then how many are the deceived!

Congedo. My 'Against-the-erring', off you go! And when you come to where my lady dwells, don't hide your mission from her: you can tell her with all confidence: 'I speak of your friend.'

70

1. Since Love has completely abandoned me—not by my choice, for never had I been so happy, but because he took such pity on my heart that he could not bear to listen to its weeping—I will direct my song, thus devoid of love as I am, against the error which has arisen amongst us of misnaming something which is base and boorish by giving it a name connoting goodness, that is by calling it Charm—a thing so fair as to make him in

che fa degno di manto
imperïal colui dov'ella regna:
ell'è verace insegna   15
la qual dimostra u' la vertù dimora;
per ch'io son certo, se ben la difendo
nel dir com'io la 'ntendo,
ch'Amor di sé mi farà grazia ancora.

Sono che per gittar via loro avere   20
credon potere
capere   là dove li boni stanno,
che dopo morte fanno
riparo ne la mente
a quei cotanti c'hanno canoscenza.   25
Ma lor messione a' bon non pò piacere;
per che tenere
savere   fora, e fuggiriano il danno,
che si aggiugne a lo 'nganno
di loro e de la gente   30
c'hanno falso iudicio in lor sentenza.
Qual non dirà fallenza
divorar cibo ed a lussuria intendere?
ornarsi, come vendere
si dovesse al mercato di non saggi?   35
ché 'l saggio non pregia om per vestimenta,
ch'altrui sono ornamenta,
ma pregia il senno e li genti coraggi.

E altri son che, per esser ridenti,
d'intendimenti   40
correnti   voglion esser iudicati
da quei che so' ingannati
veggendo rider cosa
che lo 'ntelletto cieco non la vede.

whom it reigns fit for an emperor's mantle. It is a sure sign of indwelling virtue; and so I am certain that if I defend it well, by declaring how I conceive it, Love will be gracious to me once more.

2. There are those who think that to dissipate their wealth is the way to win a place with the worthy who after death continue to dwell in the minds of such as are wise. But their extravagance cannot meet with good men's approval; so that they would be wiser to keep their cash and thus avoid also the loss which is added to their illusion—theirs and that of those whose opinion of them shows false judgement. Who will not call it folly to guzzle and give oneself over to lechery? To deck oneself out as though one were up for sale at Vanity Fair? For the wise do not esteem a man for his clothes, which are outward adornments, but for intelligence and nobility of heart.

3. Then there are others who are always laughing, because they want people to think them quick-witted—people, that is, who are deluded on seeing them laugh at something which their own dim minds don't understand.

E' parlan con vocaboli eccellenti; 45
vanno spiacenti,
contenti   che da lunga sian mirati;
non sono innamorati
mai di donna amorosa;
ne' parlamenti lor tengono scede; 50
   non moveriano il piede
per donneare a guisa di leggiadro,
ma come al furto il ladro,
così vanno a pigliar villan diletto;
e non però che 'n donne è sì dispento 55
leggiadro portamento,
che paiono animai sanza intelletto.

   Ancor che ciel con cielo in punto sia,
che leggiadria
disvia   cotanto, e più che quant'io conto, 60
io, che le sono conto
merzé d'una gentile
che la mostrava in tutti gli atti sui,
   non tacerò di lei, ché villania
far mi parria 65
sì ria,   ch'a' suoi nemici sarei giunto:
per che da questo punto
con rima più sottile
tratterò il ver di lei, ma non so cui.
   Eo giuro per colui 70
ch'Amor si chiama ed è pien di salute,
che sanza ovrar vertute
nessun pote acquistar verace loda:
dunque, se questa mia matera è bona,
come ciascun ragiona, 75
sarà vertù o con vertù s'annoda.

They speak with affected refinement, go about giving themselves airs, happy to be admired at a distance. They never love any lady whose heart is given to love. In conversation they are tediously facetious. Never would they stir themselves to court ladies in a civilized way, but like a thief to his theft they go to snatch gross pleasures; and this not because charming manners have so completely died out among women that they appear mindless animals.

4. Although the heavens are in such a conjunction that Charm has gone so far astray—and more than I have described—nevertheless, since I am familiar with Charm, thanks to a gentle lady who showed it in all she did, I will not keep silence on it, for that would seem to me so vilely ignoble as to place me among its enemies. Hence, from now on, with more subtle rhymes, I will set down the truth concerning it—though for whom I do not know. I swear by him who is called Love and who abounds in perfection, that no one can win true praise without practising virtue: therefore, if this my subject-matter is something good—as all say it is—then it must be either virtue or connected with virtue.

Non è pura vertù la disvïata,
poi ch'è blasmata,
negata   là 'v'è più vertù richesta,
cioè in gente onesta   80
di vita spiritale
o in abito che di scïenza tiene.
    Dunque, s'ell'è in cavalier lodata,
sarà mischiata,
causata   di più cose; per che questa   85
conven che di sé vesta
l'un bene e l'altro male,
ma vertù pura in ciascuno sta bene.
    Sollazzo è che convene
con esso Amore e l'opera perfetta: 90
da questo terzo retta
è vera leggiadria e in esser dura,
sì come il sole al cui esser s'adduce
lo calore e la luce
con la perfetta sua bella figura.   95

    Al gran pianeto è tutta simigliante
che, dal levante
avante   infino a tanto che s'asconde,
co li bei raggi infonde
vita e vertù qua giuso   100
ne la matera sì com'è disposta:
    e questa, disdegnosa di cotante
persone, quante
sembiante   portan d'omo, e non responde
il lor frutto a le fronde   105
per lo mal c'hanno in uso,
simili beni al cor gentile accosta;

144

5. This errant quality is not simply virtue, since it is blamed, even excluded, there where virtue is especially called for—that is, in people of dignity in the spiritual life or whose bent and disposition is learning. Therefore, if Charm is praised in a gentleman, it must be something heterogeneous, caused by several factors: and this is why it must clothe one man well, another badly, whereas simple virtue is becoming in everybody. There is a joy that concurs with love and with perfect behaviour: by these three is true Charm governed, and, so governed, it can endure; like the sun, in whose being concur heat and light and its perfect and beautiful shape.

6. Charm is like the great planet in all ways: from its rising onwards to its setting the planet pours down life and power with its fair beams into matter here below according as this is disposed to receive them; and so too Charm, disdaining all those who have the outward appearance of human beings but whose fruit does not correspond to their leaves—because of their evil ways—brings like good things to the heart that is noble; being

ché 'n donar vita è tosta
co' bei sembianti e co' begli atti novi
ch'ognora par che trovi,   110
e vertù per essemplo a chi lei piglia.
Oh falsi cavalier, malvagi e rei,
nemici di costei,
ch'al prenze de le stelle s'assimiglia!

Dona e riceve l'om cui questa vole,   115
mai non sen dole;
né 'l sole   per donar luce a le stelle,
né per prender da elle
nel suo effetto aiuto;
ma l'uno e l'altro in ciò diletto tragge.   120
    Già non s'induce a ira per parole,
ma quelle sole
ricole   che son bone, e sue novelle
sono leggiadre e belle;
per sé caro è tenuto   125
e disïato da persone sagge,
    ché de l'altre selvagge
cotanto laude quanto biasmo prezza;
per nessuna grandezza
monta in orgoglio, ma quando gl'incontra   130
che sua franchezza li conven mostrare,
quivi si fa laudare.
Color che vivon fanno tutti contra.

71 (B.LXXXVI)

Due donne in cima de la mente mia
venute sono a ragionar d'amore:
l'una ha in sé cortesia e valore,
prudenza e onestà in compagnia;

swift to give life with gracious looks and the gracious behaviour it seems to discover afresh at every moment, and swift to give virtue to those who take Charm as their model. O pseudo-gentlemen, vicious and depraved, enemies of this quality which resembles the prince of the stars!

7. The man chosen by Charm will both give and receive and never be sad at so doing, no more than the sun is sad at giving light to the stars or at receiving their assistance to bring about its effects; all this is a delight both for him and it. He will never be provoked to anger by words, for he only pays heed to those that are worth attention, and his own talk is charming and pleasant. He is held dear and his company desired for his own sake by people of good judgement; and as for the herd, he values their praise just as much as their blame. No honours can make him proud; but on the occasions when it befits him to show his free spirit, then he wins praise. The present generation, without exception, do just the reverse.

71

Two women have come to the summit of my mind to speak of love. One is accompanied by courtesy and goodness, moral wisdom and decorum; the other has beauty

l'altra ha bellezza e vaga leggiadria,   5
adorna gentilezza le fa onore:
e io, merzé del dolce mio signore,
mi sto a piè de la lor signoria.

Parlan Bellezza e Virtù a l'intelletto,
e fan quistion come un cor puote stare   10
intra due donne con amor perfetto.

Risponde il fonte del gentil parlare
ch'amar si può bellezza per diletto,
e puossi amar virtù per operare.

72 (B.LXXIII)

DANTE A FORESE DONATI

Chi udisse tossir la malfatata
moglie di Bicci vocato Forese,
potrebbe dir ch'ell'ha forse vernata
ove si fa 'l cristallo, in quel paese.

Di mezzo agosto la truove infreddata: 5
or sappi che de' far d'ogni altro mese!
e non le val perché dorma calzata,
merzé del copertoio c'ha cortonese....

La tosse, 'l freddo e l'altra mala voglia
non l'addovien per omor ch'abbia vecchi,   10
ma per difetto ch'ella sente al nido.

Piange la madre, c'ha più d'una doglia,
dicendo: 'Lassa, che per fichi secchi
messa l'avre' 'n casa del conte Guido!'

148

and lovely charm, and fair nobility does her honour. And I—thanks to my dear Lord—I kneel at their lady-ships' feet.

Beauty and Virtue speak to my intellect, debating the question how a heart can be divided between two ladies with perfect love. The source of noble speech pronounces thus: beauty can be loved for delight and virtue for the sake of action.

72

DANTE TO FORESE DONATI

Anyone who heard the coughing of the luckless wife of Bicci (called Forese) might say that maybe she'd passed the winter in the land where crystal is made. You'll find her frozen in mid-August—so guess how she must fare in any other month! And it's no use her keeping her stockings on—the bedclothes are too short. . . .

The coughing and cold and other troubles—these don't come to her from ageing humours, but from the gap she feels in the nest. Her mother, who has more than one affliction, weeps saying: 'Alas, for dried figs I could have married her to Count Guido!'

72a (B. LXXIV)

FORESE A DANTE

L'altra notte mi venne una gran tosse,
perch'i' non avea che tener a dosso;
ma incontanente che fu dì, fui mosso
per gir a guadagnar ove che fosse.

Udite la fortuna ove m'addosse: 5
ch'i' credetti trovar perle in un bosso
e be' fiorin coniati d'oro rosso;
ed i' trovai Alaghier tra le fosse,

legato a nodo ch'i' non saccio 'l nome,
se fu di Salamone o d'altro saggio.   10
Allora mi segna' verso 'l levante:

e que' mi disse: 'Per amor di Dante,
scio' mi.' Ed i' non potti veder come:
tornai a dietro, e compie' mi' vïaggio.

73 (B. LXXV)

DANTE A FORESE

Ben ti faranno il nodo Salamone,
Bicci novello, e' petti de le starne,
ma peggio fia la lonza del castrone,
ché 'l cuoio farà vendetta de la carne;

tal che starai più presso a San Simone,   5
se tu non ti procacci de l'andarne:
e 'ntendi che 'l fuggire el mal boccone
sarebbe oramai tardi a ricomprarne.

Ma ben m'è detto che tu sai un'arte
che, s'egli è vero, tu ti puoi rifare,   10
però ch'ell'è di molto gran guadagno;

FORESE DONATI TO DANTE

The other night I had a great fit of coughing, because
I'd nothing to put over me; but as soon as day came
I went off to look for money, wherever it might be found.
Hear where luck led me! For I thought I'd find pearls in
a wooden box and fine coined florins of red gold, but
I found Alighieri among the graves, tied by some knot—
I don't know if the one called Solomon's, or some other
sage's. Then I made the sign of the cross facing east. And
he said to me: 'For the love of Dante, release me.' But
I couldn't see how—so turned back and came home.

73

DANTE TO FORESE

Partridge breasts, young Bicci, will truss you in Solomon's
knot all right! But loins of mutton will be still worse for
you, for the skin will take revenge for the flesh! So much
so that you'll live a bit nearer San Simone, if you don't
hurry and get away. And by now, mind, it's too late to
redeem your debts by giving up guzzling.

But to be sure, I've been told you have a profession
with which (if this be true) you can set yourself up again;
for it's highly profitable; and it provides, for a time, that

e fa sì, a tempo, che tema di carte
non hai, che ti bisogni scioperare;
ma ben ne colse male a’ fi’ di Stagno.

73a (B.LXXVI)

FORESE A DANTE

Va’ rivesti San Gal prima che dichi
parole o motti d’altrui povertate,
ché troppo n’è venuta gran pietate
in questo verno a tutti suoi amichi.

E anco, se tu ci hai per sì mendichi,   5
perché pur mandi a noi per caritate?
Dal castello Altrafonte ha’ ta’ grembiate
ch’io saccio ben che tu te ne nutrichi.

Ma ben ti lecerà il lavorare,
se Dio ti salvi la Tana e ’l Francesco,   10
che col Belluzzo tu non stia in brigata.

A lo spedale a Pinti ha’ riparare;
e già mi par vedere stare a desco,
ed in terzo, Alighier co la farsata.

74 (B.LXXVII)

DANTE A FORESE

Bicci novel, figliuol di non so cui,
s’i’ non ne domandasse monna Tessa,
giù per la gola tanta roba hai messa,
ch’a forza ti convien torre l’altrui.

E già la gente si guarda da lui,   5
chi ha borsa a lato, là dov’e’ s’appressa,
dicendo: ‘Questi c’ha la faccia fessa
è piùvico ladron negli atti sui.’

you won't fear the bills that might put you out of action:
but certainly, no good came of it to Stagno's sons!

73a

FORESE TO DANTE

Go and pay back San Gallo before you talk or joke about
other people's poverty; for all its friends, this winter,
have been greatly troubled about it. What's more, if you
think us such beggars, why go on asking us for charity?
You have filled your lap so full at the castle of Altrafonte that I've no doubt you live on what you get there.

But God keep Tana and Francesco for you, that you
may find it possible to escape Belluzzo's company!
You'll end up in the Pinti poorhouse. And already I seem
to see you sitting at table, one of three, an Alighieri with
nothing on but a doublet.

74

DANTE TO FORESE

Young Bicci, son of I don't know who (short of asking
my lady Tessa), you've stuffed so much down your gorge
that you're driven to take from others. And already
people who carry purses keep clear of him when he
draws near, saying: 'Scarface there is obviously a known
thief.'

E tal giace per lui nel letto tristo,
per tema non sia preso a lo 'mbolare,   10
che gli appartien quanto Giosepp' a Cristo.

Di Bicci e de' fratei posso contare
che, per lo sangue lor, del male acquisto
sanno a lor donne buon cognati stare.

74a (B.LXXVIII)

FORESE A DANTE

Ben so che fosti figliuol d'Alaghieri,
ed accorgomen pur a la vendetta
che facesti di lui sì bella e netta
de l'aguglin ched e' cambiò l'altr'ieri.

Se tagliato n'avessi uno a quartieri,   5
di pace non dovevi aver tal fretta;
ma tu ha' poi sì piena la bonetta,
che non la porterebber duo somieri.

Buon uso ci ha' recato, ben til dico,
che qual ti carica ben di bastone,   10
colui ha' per fratello e per amico.

Il nome ti direi de le persone
che v'hanno posto su; ma del panico
mi reca, ch'i' vo' metter la ragione.

75a (B.XCII)

IGNOTO A DANTE

Dante Alleghier, d'ogni senno pregiato
che in corpo d'om si potesse trovare,
un tuo amico di debile affare
da la tua parte s'era richiamato

a una donna, che l'ha sì incolpato   5
con fini spade di sottil tagliare,
che in nulla guisa ne pensa scampare,
però che' colpi han già il cor toccato.

154

And there's one who lies in bed distraught for fear that he'll be caught red-handed, who has as much to do with him as Joseph with Christ. Of Bicci and his brothers I can say that, being of that clan, they know how to use their ill-gotten gains to be good kinsmen to their wives.

74a

FORESE TO DANTE

I know you're Alighieri's son all right—I can tell that by the fine clean vengeance you took on his behalf for the money he exchanged the other day. Even if you'd hacked someone in pieces, you needn't have been in such a hurry to make peace; but then you had filled your sack so full that two pack-horses couldn't carry it.

O a fine custom you've introduced here, let me tell you: that if someone lays about you with a stick, he's your friend and brother! I could name those who have counted on your cowardice—but bring me some millet, let's settle our account!

75a

AN ANONYMOUS WRITER TO DANTE

Dante Alighieri, esteemed as having all the wisdom that may be found in a man, a friend of yours, of modest condition, had expressed a grievance to a lady, claiming support from you. But she has so struck him with sharp-edged swords that he thinks he cannot possibly survive—the blows have already reached his heart.

Onde a te cade farne alta vendetta
di quella che l'ha sì forte conquiso 10
che null'altra mai non se ne inframetta.

Delle sue condizioni io vi diviso,
ch'ell'è una leggiadra giovinetta
che porta propiamente Amor nel viso.

75 (B. XCIII)

RISPOSTA DI DANTE

Io Dante a te che m'hai così chiamato
rispondo brieve con poco pensare,
però che più non posso soprastare,
tanto m'ha 'l tuo pensier forte affannato.

Ma ben vorrei saper dove e in qual lato 5
ti richiamasti, per me ricordare:
forse che per mia lettera mandare
saresti d'ogni colpo risanato.

Ma s'ella è donna che porti anco vetta,
sì 'n ogni parte mi pare esser fiso 10
ch'ella verrà a farti gran disdetta.

Secondo detto m'hai ora, m'avviso
che ella è sì d'ogni peccato netta
come angelo che stia in paradiso.

76 (B. XCIX)

DANTE A MESSER BETTO BRUNELLESCHI

Messer Brunetto, questa pulzelletta
con esso voi si ven la pasqua a fare:
non intendete pasqua di mangiare,
ch'ella non mangia, anzi vuol esser letta.

Hence it is now up to you to take great revenge on her, for his sake whom she has so destroyed that no other woman will ever concern herself with him. As to her qualities, I tell you she is young and charming and bears Love himself in her eyes.

75

I, Dante, to whom you have appealed in this way, reply briefly, without much reflection—your distress having so grieved me that I cannot linger over it. But I would very much like to know who it was you complained to, citing me. Perhaps a letter sent from me would heal you of all your wounds.

But if the lady is still unmarried, it seems to me she'll eventually unsay all she said. From what you have just told me I believe her to be as faultless as an angel in Paradise.

76

DANTE TO BETTO BRUNELLESCHI

Messer Brunetto, this young girl comes to keep Easter with you; not, you understand, an eating Easter, for she doesn't eat, she is meant to be read. Her meaning doesn't

La sua sentenzia non richiede fretta,   5
né luogo di romor né da giullare;
anzi si vuol più volte lusingare
prima che 'n intelletto altrui si metta.

Se voi non la intendete in questa guisa,
in vostra gente ha molti frati Alberti   10
da intender ciò ch'è posto loro in mano.

Con lor vi restringete sanza risa;
e se li altri de' dubbi non son certi,
ricorrete a la fine a messer Giano.

77 (B.C)

Io son venuto al punto de la rota
che l'orizzonte, quando il sol si corca,
ci partorisce il geminato cielo,
    e la stella d'amor ci sta remota
per lo raggio lucente che la 'nforca   5
sì di traverso, che le si fa velo;
    e quel pianeta che conforta il gelo
si mostra tutto a noi per lo grand'arco
nel qual ciascun di sette fa poca ombra:
e però non disgombra   10
un sol penser d'amore, ond'io son carco,
la mente mia, ch'è più dura che petra
in tener forte imagine di petra.

    Levasi de la rena d'Etïopia
lo vento peregrin che l'aere turba,   15
per la spera del sol ch'ora la scalda;
    e passa il mare, onde conduce copia
di nebbia tal, che, s'altro non la sturba,
questo emisperio chiude tutto e salda;

call for hasty reading, or a place that's noisy, or where players perform; in fact she'll require to be coaxed more than once before she'll enter a man's understanding.

And if you don't understand her in this way, there are many brother Alberts in your company to understand whatever's put into their hands. Get together with them, but without laughing; and if none of them are clear about the difficult bits, in the last resort go and ask Messer Giano.

77

1. I have come to that point on the wheel when the horizon, once the sun goes down, brings forth the twinned heaven for us; and the star of love is removed from us by the shining beam which so rides across it as to veil it away; and the planet that intensifies the cold stands fully revealed to us along the great arc in which each of the seven casts the shortest shadow. And yet my mind does not shake off a single one of the thoughts of love that burden me—my mind that is harder than *stone* in strongly retaining an image of *stone*.

2. The pilgrim wind that darkens the air rises from the sands of Ethiopia, now heated by the sun's sphere; and crossing the sea, it brings up such quantity of cloud that, unless dispersed by another wind, the cloud-mass encloses and blocks up all our hemisphere; and then it

e poi si solve, e cade in bianca falda   20
di fredda neve ed in noiosa pioggia,
onde l'aere s'attrista tutto e piagne:
e Amor, che sue ragne
ritira in alto pel vento che poggia,
non m'abbandona; sì è bella donna   25
questa crudel che m'è data per donna.

Fuggito è ogne augel che 'l caldo segue
del paese d'Europa, che non perde
le sette stelle gelide unquemai;
    e li altri han posto a le lor voci triegue   30
per non sonarle infino al tempo verde,
se ciò non fosse per cagion di guai;
    e tutti li animali che son gai
di lor natura, son d'amor disciolti,
però che 'l freddo lor spirito ammorta: 35
e 'l mio più d'amor porta;
ché li dolzi pensier non mi son tolti
né mi son dati per volta di tempo,
ma donna li mi dà c'ha picciol tempo.

Passato hanno lor termine le fronde   40
che trasse fuor la vertù d'Arïete
per adornare il mondo, e morta è l'erba;
    ramo di foglia verde a noi s'asconde
se non se in lauro, in pino o in abete
o in alcun che sua verdura serba;   45
    e tanto è la stagion forte ed acerba,
c'ha morti li fioretti per le piagge,
li quai non poten tollerar la brina:
e la crudele spina
però Amor di cor non la mi tragge;   50
per ch'io son fermo di portarla sempre
ch'io sarò in vita, s'io vivesse sempre.

dissolves and falls in white flakes of chill snow and dreary rain, so that all the air grows sad and weeps. And yet Love, who draws his nets aloft with the soaring wind, still does not leave me, so fair is this cruel *lady* who is given me as *lady*.

3. Every bird that follows the warmth has fled from the European lands which never lose the seven freezing stars; and the rest have imposed a truce on their tongues, and will make no sound until the green season, unless it be to lament; and all the beasts that are lusty by nature are released from love, for the cold numbs their spirit. And yet my spirit is more full of love than ever; for sweet thoughts are neither taken from me, nor given, with changes of *season*, but a woman gives them who has lived but a short *season*.

4. The leaves brought forth by the power of the Ram to adorn the world have passed their term, and the grass is dead; branches green with leaf are taken from our sight, save in bay or pine or fir, or in other trees that retain their leaf; and so harsh and bitter is the season, it has killed the frail flowers of the field, unable to withstand the frost. And yet Love will not draw from my heart his cruel thorn; so that I am resolved to bear it *ever*, all life long, though I were to live for *ever*.

Versan le vene le fummifere acque
per li vapor che la terra ha nel ventre,
che d'abisso li tira suso in alto;   55
    onde cammino al bel giorno mi piacque
che ora è fatto rivo, e sarà mentre
che durerà del verno il grande assalto;
    la terra fa un suol che par di smalto,
e l'acqua morta si converte in vetro   60
per la freddura che di fuor la serra:
e io de la mia guerra
non son però tornato un passo a retro,
né vo' tornar; ché, se 'l martiro è dolce,
la morte de' passare ogni altro dolce.   65

    Canzone, or che sarà di me ne l'altro
dolce tempo novello, quando piove
amore in terra da tutti li cieli,
quando per questi geli
amore è solo in me, e non altrove?   70
Saranne quello ch'è d'un uom di marmo,
se in pargoletta fia per core un marmo.

78 (B. CI)

Al poco giorno e al gran cerchio d'ombra
son giunto, lasso, ed al bianchir de' colli,
quando si perde lo color ne l'erba:
e 'l mio disio però non cangia il verde,
sì è barbato ne la dura petra   5
che parla e sente come fosse donna.

    Similemente questa nova donna
si sta gelata come neve a l'ombra;
ché non la move, se non come petra,
il dolce tempo che riscalda i colli,   10
e che li fa tornar di bianco in verde
perché li copre di fioretti e d'erba.

5. The springs spew forth fumy waters because the earth draws the gases that are in its bowels upwards from the abyss; so that a path that pleased me in fine weather is now a stream, and so will remain as long as winter's great onslaught endures; the earth has formed a crust like rock and the dead waters turn into glass because of the cold that locks them in. And yet I have not withdrawn one step from the struggle, nor will I withdraw; for if suffering be *sweet*, death must be *sweet* above all things.

Congedo. My song, what will become of me in that other, that sweet young season when love pours down to the earth from all the heavens; if love, amid all this cold, is found only in me and nowhere else? It will be with me as with a man of *marble*, if a girl keeps a heart of *marble*.

78

1. To the short day and the great circle of *shadow* I have come, alas, and to the whitening of the *hills*, when the *grass* loses its colour: and yet my desire remains ever-green, it is so rooted in the hard *stone* which speaks and has senses like a *woman*.

2. This young *woman* stays frozen like snow in *shadow*; for the sweet season moves her no more than *stone*, the season that warms the *hills* and turns them from white to green, covering them with flowers and *grass*.

Quand'ella ha in testa una ghirlanda d'erba,
trae de la mente nostra ogn'altra donna;
perché si mischia il crespo giallo e 'l verde   15
sì bel, ch'Amor lì viene a stare a l'ombra,
che m'ha serrato intra piccioli colli
più forte assai che la calcina petra.

La sua bellezza ha più vertù che petra,
e 'l colpo suo non può sanar per erba;   20
ch'io son fuggito per piani e per colli,
per potere scampar da cotal donna;
e dal suo lume non mi può far ombra
poggio né muro mai né fronda verde.

Io l'ho veduta già vestita a verde,   25
sì fatta ch'ella avrebbe messo in petra
l'amor ch'io porto pur a la sua ombra:
ond'io l'ho chesta in un bel prato d'erba,
innamorata com'anco fu donna,
e chiuso intorno d'altissimi colli.   30

Ma ben ritorneranno i fiumi a' colli,
prima che questo legno molle e verde
s'infiammi, come suol far bella donna,
di me; che mi torrei dormire in petra
tutto il mio tempo e gir pascendo l'erba,   35
sol per veder do' suoi panni fanno ombra.

Quandunque i colli fanno più nera ombra,
sotto un bel verde la giovane donna
la fa sparer, com'uom petra sott'erba.

3. When she wears on her head a garland of *grass* she takes every other *woman* from our mind; for the curling yellow and the *green* mingle so beautifully that Love comes to dwell in their *shadow*, Love who has locked me between small *hills* more tightly than cement locks *stone*.

4. Her beauty has more power than *stone*, nor can her blows be healed by *grass*: and I have fled over plains and *hills* to escape, if possible, from such a *woman*; but from her light I can find no *shadow* under mountain or wall or *green* bough.

5. I once saw her clothed in *green* and such that she would have imparted to *stone* the love I bear to her mere *shadow*; hence I have desired her in a fair *grass* field—as much in love as ever a *woman* was—enclosed by great *hills*.

6. But surely rivers will return to the *hills* before this wet *green* wood catches fire, as is the way of fair *woman*, for me—who would consent to sleep on *stone* all my days and go about eating *grass*, only to see where her dress casts a *shadow*.

Whenever the *hills* cast darkest *shadow* this young *woman* makes it disappear beneath a fair *green*, as one makes *stone* disappear under *grass*.

79 <small>(B. CII)</small>

Amor, tu vedi ben che questa donna
la tua vertù non cura in alcun tempo,
che suol de l'altre belle farsi donna;
e poi s'accorse ch'ell'era mia donna
per lo tuo raggio ch'al volto mi luce,   5
d'ogne crudelità si fece donna;
   sì che non par ch'ell'abbia cor di donna
ma di qual fiera l'ha d'amor più freddo;
ché per lo tempo caldo e per lo freddo
mi fa sembiante pur come una donna   10
che fosse fatta d'una bella petra
per man di quei che me' intagliasse in petra.

   E io, che son costante più che petra
in ubidirti per bieltà di donna,
porto nascoso il colpo de la petra,   15
con la qual tu mi desti come a petra
che t'avesse innoiato lungo tempo,
tal che m'andò al core ov'io son petra.
   E mai non si scoperse alcuna petra
o da splendor di sole o da sua luce,   20
che tanta avesse né vertù né luce
che mi potesse atar da questa petra,
sì ch'ella non mi meni col suo freddo
colà dov'io sarò di morte freddo.

   Segnor, tu sai che per algente freddo   25
l'acqua diventa cristallina petra
là sotto tramontana ov'è il gran freddo,
e l'aere sempre in elemento freddo
vi si converte, sì che l'acqua è donna
in quella parte per cagion del freddo: 30

79

1. Love, you see well that this *lady* at no *time* heeds your force which usually becomes *lady* of other fair women. And when she saw that she was my *lady*, by your beam's *light* on my face, she became *lady* of all cruelty, so that she seems to have a heart, not of a *lady*, but of whatever wild beast has its heart most *cold* to love : for through the hot season and the *cold* she shows me always the likeness of a *lady* made of beautiful *stone* by hand of the man who carves best in *stone*.

2. And I who am firmer than *stone* in obeying you for the sake of a *lady*'s beauty, bear concealed the blow of that *stone* with which you struck me, as though at a *stone* that had a long *time* irked you, with a blow such that it went to my heart where I am become *stone*. And no *stone* has ever been discovered, whether through reflected sunlight or through its own *light*, that would have sufficient power or *light* to help me against that *stone*, to prevent its leading me with its *cold* to where I shall be *cold* in death.

3. Lord, you know that through freezing *cold* the water becomes crystal *stone*, there in the north where the great *cold* is; and there the air is perpetually changing into the *cold* element, so that there water is *lady* because of the *cold*;

così dinanzi dal sembiante freddo
mi ghiaccia sopra il sangue d'ogne tempo,
e quel pensiero che m'accorcia il tempo
mi si converte tutto in corpo freddo,
che m'esce poi per mezzo de la luce   35
là ond'entrò la dispietata luce.

In lei s'accoglie d'ogni bieltà luce;
così di tutta crudeltate il freddo
le corre al core, ove non va tua luce:
per che ne li occhi sì bella mi luce   40
quando la miro, ch'io la veggio in petra,
e po' in ogni altro ov'io volga mia luce.
    Da li occhi suoi mi ven la dolce luce
che mi fa non caler d'ogn'altra donna:
così foss'ella più pietosa donna   45
ver me, che chiamo di notte e di luce,
solo per lei servire, e luogo e tempo!
Né per altro disio viver gran tempo.

Però, vertù che se' prima che tempo,
prima che moto o che sensibil luce,   50
increscati di me, c'ho sì mal tempo;
entrale in core omai, ché ben n'è tempo,
sì che per te se n'esca fuor lo freddo
che non mi lascia aver, com'altri, tempo:
    ché se mi giunge lo tuo forte tempo   55
in tale stato, questa gentil petra
mi vedrà coricare in poca petra,
per non levarmi se non dopo il tempo,
quando vedrò se mai fu bella donna
nel mondo come questa acerba donna.   60

likewise, in the presence of that *cold* face my blood at all *times* freezes and that thought which shortens my *time* is all changed into a *cold* body, which then issues from me by way of the *light* through which the pitiless *light* entered.

4. The *light* of all beauty is gathered in her, and so too the *cold* of all cruelty runs to her heart where your *light* does not reach. And therefore she is *alight* in my eyes with such beauty when I look at her, that I see her in *stone* and everywhere I then turn my *light*. From her eyes comes the sweet *light* which makes me heedless of every other *lady*: would that she were a more merciful *lady* towards me who beg in the night and in the *light* only place and *time* to serve her: and for nothing else do I desire to live for a long *time*.

5. Therefore, O Power that exists before *time*, before motion or corporeal *light*, have pity on me whose *time* is so wretched; enter her heart at last, for it is high *time*, so that by your agency the *cold* may come out of it which does not permit me to have, as others do, my allotted *time*: for if the *time* of your strength comes upon me while in such a condition, this noble *stone* will see me lie down in a small *stone* never to rise until after *time*, when I shall see whether there was ever in the world a *lady* so beautiful as this cruel *lady*.

Canzone, io porto ne la mente donna
tal, che, con tutto ch'ella mi sia petra,
mi dà baldanza, ond'ogni uom mi par freddo:
sì ch'io ardisco a far per questo freddo
la novità che per tua forma luce, 65
che non fu mai pensata in alcun tempo.

80 (B. CIII)

Così nel mio parlar voglio esser aspro
com'è ne li atti questa bella petra,
la quale ognora impetra
maggior durezza e più natura cruda,
e veste sua persona d'un dïaspro 5
tal, che per lui, o perch'ella s'arretra,
non esce di faretra
saetta che già mai la colga ignuda:
ed ella ancide, e non val ch'om si chiuda
né si dilunghi da' colpi mortali, 10
che, com'avesser ali,
giungono altrui e spezzan ciascun'arme;
sì ch'io non so da lei né posso atarme.

Non trovo scudo ch'ella non mi spezzi
né loco che dal suo viso m'asconda; 15
ché, come fior di fronda,
così de la mia mente tien la cima.
Cotanto del mio mal par che si prezzi
quanto legno di mar che non lieva onda;
e 'l peso che m'affonda 20
è tal che non potrebbe adequar rima.
Ahi angosciosa e dispietata lima
che sordamente la mia vita scemi,
perché non ti ritemi
sì di rodermi il core a scorza a scorza, 25
com'io di dire altrui chi ti dà forza?

Song, I bear in my mind a *lady* such that, though she is a *stone* to me, she gives me such boldness that all men to me seem *cold*; so that I dare to create for this *cold* object the novelty that is *alight* through your form, a thing never conceived before at any *time*.

80

1. I want to be as harsh in my speech as this fair stone is in her behaviour—she who at every moment acquires greater hardness and a crueller nature, and arms her body with jasper such that, because of it, or because she retreats, no arrow ever came from quiver that could catch her unprotected. But she is a killer, and it is no use putting on armour or fleeing from her deadly blows, which find their target as though they had wings and shatter one's every weapon; so that I've neither the skill nor the strength to defend myself from her.

2. I cannot find a shield that she does not shatter, nor a place to hide from her face; for like a flower on its stalk so she holds the crest of my mind. She heeds my misery no more than a ship heeds a sea that lifts no wave; and the weight that sinks me is such that no verse would suffice to describe it. Ah, agonizing merciless file that hiddenly rasps my life away! Why do you not refrain from so gnawing my heart through layer by layer, as I do from revealing who she is who gives you strength?

Ché più mi triema il cor qualora io penso
di lei in parte ov'altri li occhi induca,
per tema non traluca
lo mio penser di fuor sì che si scopra, 30
    ch'io non fo de la morte, che ogni senso
co li denti d'Amor già mi manduca;
ciò è che 'l pensier bruca
la lor vertù, sì che n'allenta l'opra.

    E' m'ha percosso in terra, e stammi sopra 35
con quella spada ond'elli ancise Dido,
Amore, a cui io grido
merzé chiamando, e umilmente il priego;
ed el d'ogni merzé par messo al niego.

    Egli alza ad ora ad or la mano, e sfida 40
la debole mia vita, esto perverso,
che disteso a riverso
mi tiene in terra d'ogni guizzo stanco:
    allor mi surgon ne la mente strida;
e 'l sangue, ch'è per le vene disperso, 45
fuggendo corre verso
lo cor, che 'l chiama; ond'io rimango bianco.
    Elli mi fiede sotto il braccio manco
sì forte, che 'l dolor nel cor rimbalza:
allor dico: 'S'elli alza 50
un'altra volta, Morte m'avrà chiuso
prima che 'l colpo sia disceso giuso.'

    Così vedess'io lui fender per mezzo
lo core a la crudele che 'l mio squatra!
poi non mi sarebb'atra 55
la morte, ov'io per sua bellezza corro:
    ché tanto dà nel sol quanto nel rezzo
questa scherana micidiale e latra.
Omè, perché non latra
per me, com'io per lei, nel caldo borro? 60

3. For whenever I think of her in a place where another may turn his eyes, my heart trembles more with fear lest my thought shine out and be discovered, than I tremble at that death which already is devouring all my senses with the teeth of Love; that is, my torment is gnawing away their strength and slowing down their action. Love has struck me to the ground and stands over me with the sword with which he slew Dido, and I cry to him calling for mercy, and humbly I implore him, but he shows himself set against all mercy.

4. Again and again he raises his hand threatening my weakened life, this evil one who pins me to the ground, flat on my back, and too exhausted to move. Then shrieks arise in my mind, and the blood that was dispersed through my veins runs fleeing back to the heart that summons it, so that I am left white. He strikes me under the left arm so violently that the pain rebounds through my heart. Then I say: 'If he lifts his hand again, death will have locked me in before the blow descends.'

5. Would that I could see him split the heart of the cruel woman who cuts mine to pieces! For then that death would not seem black to me, to which her beauty drives me—striking as she does with equal force in sunlight and in shade, this murderous assassin and robber. Alas, why does she not howl for me in the hot gorge,

ché tosto griderei: 'Io vi soccorro';
e fare' l volentier, sì come quelli
che ne' biondi capelli
ch'Amor per consumarmi increspa e dora
metterei mano, e piacere'le allora.   65

S'io avessi le belle trecce prese,
che fatte son per me scudiscio e ferza,
pigliandole anzi terza,
con esse passerei vespero e squille:
    e non sarei pietoso né cortese,   70
anzi farei com'orso quando scherza;
e se Amor me ne sferza,
io mi vendicherei di più di mille.
    Ancor ne li occhi, ond'escon le faville
che m'infiammano il cor, ch'io porto anciso,   75
guarderei presso e fiso,
per vendicar lo fuggir che mi face;
e poi le renderei con amor pace.

Canzon, vattene dritto a quella donna
che m'ha ferito il core e che m'invola   80
quello ond'io ho più gola,
e dàlle per lo cor d'una saetta:
ché bell'onor s'acquista in far vendetta.

81 (B. CIV)

Tre donne intorno al cor mi son venute,
e seggonsi di fore;
ché dentro siede Amore,
lo quale è in segnoria de la mia vita.
    Tanto son belle e di tanta vertute,   5
che 'l possente segnore,
dico quel ch'è nel core,
a pena del parlar di lor s'aita.

174

as I do for her? For at once I'd cry: 'I'll help you': and gladly would I do so, for in the yellow hair that Love curls and gilds for my destruction I'd put my hand, and then she would begin to love me.

6. Once I'd taken in my hand the fair locks which have become my whip and lash, seizing them before terce I'd pass through vespers with them and the evening bell: and I'd not show pity or courtesy, O no, I'd be like a bear at play. And though Love whips me with them now, I would take my revenge more than a thousandfold. Still more, I'd gaze into those eyes whence come the sparks that inflame my heart which is dead within me; I'd gaze into them close and fixedly, to revenge myself on her for fleeing from me as she does: and then with love I would make our peace.

Congedo. Song, go straight to that woman who has wounded my heart and robs me of what I most hunger for, and drive an arrow through her heart: for great honour is gained through taking revenge.

81

1. Three women have come round my heart, and sit outside it, for within sits Love who holds sway over my life. They are so beautiful and of such dignity that the mighty Lord, I mean him in my heart, almost shrinks

Ciascuna par dolente e sbigottita,
come persona discacciata e stanca,   10
cui tutta gente manca
e cui vertute né beltà non vale.
Tempo fu già nel quale,
secondo il lor parlar, furon dilette;
or sono a tutti in ira ed in non cale.   15
Queste così solette
venute son come a casa d'amico;
ché sanno ben che dentro è quel ch'io dico.

Dolesi l'una con parole molto,
e 'n su la man si posa   20
come succisa rosa:
il nudo braccio, di dolor colonna,
   sente l'oraggio che cade dal volto;
l'altra man tiene ascosa
la faccia lagrimosa: 25
discinta e scalza, e sol di sé par donna.
   Come Amor prima per la rotta gonna
la vide in parte che il tacere è bello,
egli, pietoso e fello,
di lei e del dolor fece dimanda.   30
'Oh di pochi vivanda',
rispose in voce con sospiri mista,
'nostra natura qui a te ci manda:
io, che son la più trista,
son suora a la tua madre, e son Drittura;   35
povera, vedi, a panni ed a cintura.'

Poi che fatta si fu palese e conta,
doglia e vergogna prese
lo mio segnore, e chiese
chi fosser l'altre due ch'eran con lei.   40

from speech with them. They each seem sorrowful and dismayed, like those driven from home and weary, abandoned by all, their virtue and beauty being of no avail. There was a time, to judge from their account, when they were loved: now all regard them with hostility or indifference. All alone, then, they have come as to the house of a friend, for they know well that he of whom I speak is here.

2. One of them begins to lament bitterly, resting her head on her hand like a clipped rose: her bare arm, a column for grief, feels the rain that falls from her eyes; her other hand conceals the tear-stained face: ungirt and barefoot, only in her person does she reveal herself a lady. When Love first saw, through the torn dress, that part of her which it is decent not to name, in pity and anger he asked about her and her grief. 'O food of the few', she replied, her voice mingled with sighs, 'it is our kinship that makes us come to you; I, who am the saddest, am sister to your mother; I am Justice—poor, as you see, in dress and girdle.'

3. When she had revealed herself and made herself known, sorrow and shame seized my lord, and he asked who were the other two with her. And she, who had

E questa, ch'era sì di pianger pronta,
tosto che lui intese,
più nel dolor s'accese,
dicendo: 'A te non duol de gli occhi miei?'
 Poi cominciò: 'Sì come saper dei,   45
di fonte nasce il Nilo picciol fiume
quivi dove 'l gran lume
toglie a la terra del vinco la fronda:
sovra la vergin onda
generai io costei che m'è da lato   50
e che s'asciuga con la treccia bionda.
Questo mio bel portato,
mirando sé ne la chiara fontana,
generò questa che m'è più lontana.'

 Fenno i sospiri Amore un poco tardo; 55
e poi con gli occhi molli,
che prima furon folli,
salutò le germane sconsolate.
 E poi che prese l'uno e l'altro dardo,
disse: 'Drizzate i colli: 60
ecco l'armi ch'io volli;
per non usar, vedete, son turbate.
 Larghezza e Temperanza e l'altre nate
del nostro sangue mendicando vanno.
Però, se questo è danno,   65
piangano gli occhi e dolgasi la bocca
de li uomini a cui tocca,
che sono a' raggi di cotal ciel giunti;
non noi, che semo de l'etterna rocca:
ché, se noi siamo or punti,   70
noi pur saremo, e pur tornerà gente
che questo dardo farà star lucente.'

wept so readily, no sooner heard him than she kindled with yet more grief and said: 'Have you no pity on my eyes?' Then she began: 'As you surely know, the Nile springs, as a little stream, from its source there where the great light takes the osier-leaf from the earth: by the virgin wave I brought forth her who is at my side and who dries her tears with her yellow hair. She, my fair child, gazing at herself in the clear spring, brought forth her who is further from me.'

4. His sighs made Love falter a little: then, with eyes moist that before had been heedless, he greeted his unhappy kinsfolk. And then, seizing both his arrows, he said: 'Lift up your heads: here are the weapons I have chosen—weapons, you see, that are tarnished from disuse. Generosity and Temperance and the others born of our blood go begging: and yet, though this is a disaster, let the eyes that weep and the mouths that wail be those of mankind whom it concerns, having fallen under the rays of such a heaven; not ours, who are of the eternal citadel. For though we are wounded now, we shall yet live on, and a people will return that will keep this arrow bright.

E io, che ascolto nel parlar divino
consolarsi e dolersi
così alti dispersi,   75
l'essilio che m'è dato, onor mi tegno:
   ché, se giudizio o forza di destino
vuol pur che il mondo versi
i bianchi fiori in persi,
cader co' buoni è pur di lode degno.   80
   E se non che de gli occhi miei 'l bel segno
per lontananza m'è tolto dal viso,
che m'have in foco miso,
lieve mi conterei ciò che m'è grave.
Ma questo foco m'have   85
già consumato sì l'ossa e la polpa
che Morte al petto m'ha posto la chiave.
Onde, s'io ebbi colpa,
più lune ha volto il sol poi che fu spenta,
se colpa muore perché l'uom si penta.   90

   Canzone, a' panni tuoi non ponga uom mano,
per veder quel che bella donna chiude:
bastin le parti nude;
lo dolce pome a tutta gente niega,
per cui ciascun man piega.   95
Ma s'elli avvien che tu alcun mai truovi
amico di virtù, ed e' ti priega,
fatti di color novi,
poi li ti mostra; e 'l fior, ch'è bel di fori,
fa' disïar ne li amorosi cori.   100

   Canzone, uccella con le bianche penne;
canzone, caccia con li neri veltri,
che fuggir mi convenne,
ma far mi poterian di pace dono.
Però nol fan che non san quel che sono: 105
camera di perdon savio uom non serra,
ché 'l perdonare è bel vincer di guerra.

5. And I who listen to such noble exiles taking comfort and telling their grief in divine speech, I count as an honour the exile imposed on me; for if judgement or force of destiny does indeed desire that the world turn the white flowers into dark, it is still praiseworthy to fall with the good. And were it not that the fair goal of my eyes is removed by distance from my sight—and this has set me on fire—I would count as light that which weighs on me. But that fire has already so consumed my bones and flesh that Death has put his key to my breast. Even if I was to blame for it, the sun has now circled for several moons since that was cancelled, if blame dies through repentance.

Congedo (1). Song, let no man touch your dress to see what a fair woman hides; let the uncovered parts suffice; deny to all the sweet fruit for which all stretch out their hands. But should it ever happen that you find someone who's a friend to virtue, and he should ask you, put on fresh colours and then show yourself to him; and make the flower that has outward beauty be desired by hearts in love.

Congedo (2). Song, go hawking with the white wings; song, go hunting with the black hounds—which I have had to flee, though they could still make me the gift of peace. It is because they don't know what I am that they don't do so: a wise man will not lock the chamber of forgiveness; for to forgive is fine victory in war.

82 (B. C V)

Se vedi li occhi miei di pianger vaghi
per novella pietà che 'l cor mi strugge,
per lei ti priego che da te non fugge,
Signor, che tu di tal piacere i svaghi;

con la tua dritta man, cioè, che paghi   5
chi la giustizia uccide e poi rifugge
al gran tiranno, del cui tosco sugge
ch'elli ha già sparto e vuol che 'l mondo allaghi;

e messo ha di paura tanto gelo
nel cor de' tuo' fedei che ciascun tace.   10
Ma tu, foco d'amor, lume del cielo,

questa vertù che nuda e fredda giace,
levala su vestita del tuo velo,
ché sanza lei non è in terra pace.

83 (B. C VI)

Doglia mi reca ne lo core ardire
a voler ch'è di veritate amico;
però, donne, s'io dico
parole quasi contra a tutta gente,
non vi maravigliate,   5
   ma conoscete il vil vostro disire:
ché la beltà ch'Amore in voi consente,
a vertù solamente
formata fu dal suo decreto antico,
contra 'l qual voi fallate.   10

82

Lord, if you see my eyes desiring to weep because of a fresh sorrow that breaks my heart, I beg you, for the sake of her who never leaves you, that you relieve them of this desire; that is, that with your righteous hand you repay him who murders justice and then takes refuge with the great tyrant, sucking the poison which the tyrant has already poured forth in the wish that it may flood the world;

that you repay him who has cast such a chill of fear into the hearts of your faithful that all keep silence. But you, fire of love, light of heaven, raise up, clothed in your veil, this virtue which lies naked and cold; for without her there is no peace on earth.

83

1. Grief brings boldness to my heart on behalf of a desire that is friend to truth. If then, ladies, I speak against almost everyone, do not wonder at this, but recognize the baseness of your inclinations: for the beauty that Love concedes to you was created solely for virtue, according to his original decree, against which you are sinning.

Io dico a voi che siete innamorate
che, se vertute a noi
fu data, e beltà a voi,
e a costui di due potere un fare,
voi non dovreste amare,   15
ma coprir quanto di biltà v'è dato,
poi che non c'è vertù, ch'era suo segno.
Lasso, a che dicer vegno?
Dico che bel disdegno
sarebbe in donna, di ragion laudato,   20
partir beltà da sé per suo commiato.

Omo da sé vertù fatto ha lontana;
omo no, mala bestia ch'om simiglia.
O Deo, qual maraviglia
voler cadere in servo di signore,   25
o ver di vita in morte!
Vertute, al suo fattor sempre sottana,
lui obedisce e lui acquista onore,
donne, tanto che Amore
la segna d'eccellente sua famiglia   30
ne la beata corte:
lietamente esce da le belle porte,
a la sua donna torna;
lieta va e soggiorna,
lietamente ovra suo gran vassallaggio;   35
per lo corto vïaggio
conserva, adorna, accresce ciò che trova;
Morte repugna sì che lei non cura.
O cara ancella e pura,
colt'hai nel ciel misura;   40
tu sola fai segnore, e quest'è prova
che tu se' possession che sempre giova.

I say to you, women who are in love, that if virtue was granted to us, and beauty to you, and to Love the power to make of two things one, then you should love no more, but rather hide the beauty given you, since virtue, that was its goal, is found no more. Alas, what am I brought to say? I say it would be an act of fine scorn in a woman, and rightly praised, to sever beauty from herself—herself bidding it farewell.

2. Men have cut themselves off from virtue—no, not men, but evil beasts in man's likeness. O God, how strange—to choose to fall from master to slave, from life to death! Virtue, ever subject to her maker, obeys him, ladies, and wins him honour, until Love invests her as his high minister in the blessed court. With joy she comes out from the fair gates; with joy returns to her lady; with joy she travels and stays; with joy she carries out her great service; along the brief journey, she preserves, adorns, increases what she finds; she is so contrary to Death as never to heed him. O precious and pure hand-maid, it was in heaven that you found your standard: you alone confer lordship, and this proves you to be a possession that can never fail.

Servo non di signor, ma di vil servo
si fa chi da cotal serva si scosta.
Vedete quanto costa, 45
se ragionate l'uno e l'altro danno,
a chi da lei si svia:
   questo servo signor tant'è protervo,
che gli occhi ch'a la mente lume fanno
chiusi per lui si stanno, 50
sì che gir ne convene a colui posta,
ch'adocchia pur follia.
   Ma perché lo meo dire util vi sia,
discenderò del tutto
in parte, ed in costrutto 55
più lieve, sì che men grave s'intenda:
ché rado sotto benda
parola oscura giugne ad intelletto;
per che parlar con voi si vole aperto:
ma questo vo' per merto, 60
per voi, non per me certo,
ch'abbiate a vil ciascuno e a dispetto,
ché simiglianza fa nascer diletto.

   Chi è servo è come quello ch'è seguace
ratto a segnore, e non sa dove vada, 65
per dolorosa strada;
come l'avaro seguitando avere,
ch'a tutti segnoreggia.
   Corre l'avaro, ma più fugge pace:
oh mente cieca, che non pò vedere 70
lo suo folle volere
che 'l numero, ch'ognora a passar bada,
che 'nfinito vaneggia!

3. Slave of a base slave, not of a lord, he becomes who departs from such a handmaid. If you reckon up the double loss you'll see what it costs him who strays from her. That slave-lord is so arrogant that the eyes which illuminate the mind remain closed because of him, so that we are forced to walk at the whim of him who keeps his eyes fixed only on folly. But that my speech may be of use to you, I'll come down from the general to the particular, and to a simpler form of expression, so that its meaning is less hard to grasp; for seldom do obscure words reach an intellect clothed in a veil; hence with you one must speak clearly. But this I require in recompense (for your own good, to be sure, not mine) that you despise and scorn every man; for it's similarity that causes pleasure.

4. A man so enslaved is like someone following headlong after his master along a painful road without knowing where he goes; like a miser following riches, the master of all. The miser runs, only to be ever further away from peace. O blinded mind, for its insane desire cannot see that the sum which every moment it strives to pass stretches on to empty infinity! See, the one who

Ecco giunta colei che ne pareggia:
dimmi, che hai tu fatto,   75
cieco avaro disfatto?
Rispondimi, se puoi, altro che 'Nulla'.
Maladetta tua culla,
che lusingò cotanti sonni invano!
Maladetto lo tuo perduto pane,   80
che non si perde al cane!
ché da sera e da mane
hai raunato e stretto ad ambo mano
ciò che sì tosto si rifà lontano.

Come con dismisura si rauna,   85
così con dismisura si distringe:
questo è quello che pinge
molti in servaggio; e s'alcun si difende,
non è sanza gran briga.
Morte, che fai? che fai, fera Fortuna,   90
che non solvete quel che non si spende?
se 'l fate, a cui si rende?
Non so, poscia che tal cerchio ne cinge
che di là su ne riga.
Colpa è de la ragion che nol gastiga.   95
Se vol dire 'I' son presa',
ah com poca difesa
mostra segnore a cui servo sormonta!
Qui si raddoppia l'onta,
se ben si guarda là dov'io addito,   100
falsi animali, a voi ed altrui crudi,
che vedete gir nudi
per colli e per paludi
omini innanzi cui vizio è fuggito,
e voi tenete vil fango vestito.   105

makes us all equal has come. Tell me, what have you done, blind, undone miser? Answer me—if you can—other than 'Nothing'. Cursed be your cradle which beguiled so many dreams in vain; cursed be the bread you've wasted, that's not wasted on a dog; for evening and morning you have gathered and hoarded with both hands that which so quickly slips from your grasp.

5. Just as they gather immoderately, so they hoard immoderately: this is what drives many into slavery; and if any put up resistance, it is not without a great struggle. What are you doing, Death? Unfeeling Fortune, what are you doing—that you don't disperse what is left unspent? And if you were to, to whom should it go? I don't know—for there's a circle enclosing us that marks our limits from above. It's reason's fault for not correcting this: and if reason says 'I am captive'—oh, how paltry a defence a master puts up, who is over-powered by a slave! And here there is a double disgrace (if you fix your attention where I'm pointing), you false animals, cruel to yourselves and to others, who see men from whose presence vice has fled going naked over mountain and marsh, while you keep your own vile mud clothed.

Fassi dinanzi da l'avaro volto
vertù, che i suoi nimici a pace invita,
con matera pulita,
per allettarlo a sé; ma poco vale,
ché sempre fugge l'esca.   110
   Poi che girato l'ha chiamando molto,
gitta 'l pasto ver lui, tanto glien cale;
ma quei non v'apre l'ale:
e se pur vene quand'ell'è partita,
tanto par che li 'ncresca   115
   come ciò possa dar, sì che non esca
dal benefizio loda.
I' vo' che ciascun m'oda:
chi con tardare, e chi con vana vista,
chi con sembianza trista,   120
volge il donare in vender tanto caro
quanto sa sol chi tal compera paga.
Volete udir se piaga?
Tanto chi prende smaga,
che 'l negar poscia non li pare amaro.   125
Così altrui e sé concia l'avaro.

   Disvelato v'ho, donne, in alcun membro
la viltà de la gente che vi mira,
perché l'aggiate in ira;
ma troppo è più ancor quel che s'asconde   130
perché a dicerne è lado.
   In ciascun è di ciascun vizio assembro,
per che amistà nel mondo si confonde:
ché l'amorose fronde
di radice di ben altro ben tira,   135
poi sol simile è in grado.

6. Virtue, who invites her enemies to a reconciliation, appears in the miser's sight, with bright object in hand to attract him to her; but it's of little avail, for he always avoids the lure. After she has walked all round him, calling persistently, she throws the morsel towards him, so great is her concern for him; but he does not open his wings to fly to it. And if he does come for it, after she has gone, he is so greatly and obviously pained by the thought as to how he can afford the gift, that no praise results from his charity. I want all to hear me: some by delaying, some by their look of complacency, others by sullen looks, turn the gift into a sale, and at a price so high as only he knows who pays for such a purchase. Do you want to hear how it wounds? It so crushes the recipient that afterwards a refusal won't seem bitter to him. This is what the miser brings others—and himself—down to.

7. Ladies, I have partly laid bare to you the baseness of the men who admire you, that you may hold them in contempt; but far more has been left hidden, since it would be offensive to speak of it. All the vices have congregated in each one of them, and this is why mutual love in this world is all in confusion; for from a good root it takes another good to draw out the leaves of love, because only like is agreeable to like. See then how

Vedete come conchiudendo vado:
che non dee creder quella
cui par bene esser bella,
esser amata da questi cotali;   140
che se beltà tra i mali
volemo annumerar, creder si pòne,
chiamando amore appetito di fera!
Oh cotal donna pera
che sua biltà dischiera   145
da natural bontà per tal cagione,
e crede amor fuor d'orto di ragione!

Canzone, presso di qui è una donna
ch'è del nostro paese;
bella, saggia e cortese   150
la chiaman tutti, e neun se n'accorge
quando suo nome porge,
Bianca, Giovanna, Contessa chiamando:
a costei te ne va' chiusa ed onesta;
prima con lei t'arresta,   155
prima a lei manifesta
quel che tu se' e quel per ch'io ti mando;
poi seguirai secondo suo comando.

84a (B.XCIV)

MESSER CINO DA PISTOIA A DANTE

Novellamente Amor mi giura e dice
d'una donna gentil, s'i' la riguardo,
che per vertù de lo su' novo sguardo
ella sarà del meo cor bëatrice.

Io c'ho provato po' come disdice,   5
quando vede imbastito lo suo dardo,
ciò che promette, a morte mi do tardo,
ch'i' non potrò contraffar la fenice.

I conclude—that she who thinks it good to be beautiful should not believe herself loved by such as these; though if we choose to number beauty among evils, then that belief is possible—provided one gives the name 'love' to bestial appetite! O death to the woman who for such a pretext sunders her beauty from natural goodness, believing that love can be found outside the garden of reason!

Congedo. Song, nearby is a lady from our country: everyone calls her beautiful, wise, courteous; yet no one is aware of so doing when he utters her name, saying 'Bianca, Giovanna, Contessa'. Make your way to her in a modest and reserved manner; stay first with her; to her first make plain what you are and why I send you. Afterwards continue your journey as she will direct you.

84a

CINO DA PISTOIA TO DANTE

Just recently Love has told me on oath that if I look at a certain gentle lady, she with the power of her wonderful look will beatify my heart. I, who know by experience how Love, once he sees that his shaft is ready to fly, takes back his promises, I'm reluctant to die, being unable to imitate the phoenix.

S'io levo gli occhi, e del suo colpo perde
lo core mio quel poco che di vita　　　　　　　10
gli rimase d'un'altra sua ferita.

Che farò, Dante? ch'Amor pur m'invita,
e d'altra parte il tremor mi disperde
che peggio che lo scur non mi sia 'l verde.

84 (B.XCV)

RISPOSTA DI DANTE

I'ho veduto già senza radice
legno ch'è per omor tanto gagliardo,
che que' che vide nel fiume lombardo
cader suo figlio, fronde fuor n'elice;

ma frutto no, però che 'l contradice　　　　　　　5
natura, ch'al difetto fa riguardo,
perché conosce che saria bugiardo
sapor non fatto da vera notrice.

Giovane donna a cotal guisa verde
talor per gli occhi sì a dentro è gita　　　　　　　10
che tardi poi è stata la partita.

Periglio è grande in donna sì vestita:
però †lacontro† de la gente verde
parmi che la tua caccia [non] seguer de'.

85 (B.XCVI)

DANTE A MESSER CINO DA PISTOIA

Perch'io non trovo chi meco ragioni
del signor a cui siete voi ed io,
conviemmi sodisfare al gran disio
ch'i'ho di dire i pensamenti boni.

194

If I raise my eyes, at once my heart will lose, by his blow, what little life was left it by another wound it had from him. Dante, what shall I do? For Love keeps urging me on, and on the other hand the fear unnerves me that the green may prove worse than the black.

84

DANTE TO CINO

I have seen a rootless tree with such vigorous sap in it that he who saw his son fall into the Lombard river drew leaves from it—but no fruit, that being forbidden by Nature who takes account of the deficiency, knowing that the fruit's taste would be deceptive if not derived from the true nurse.

Sometimes a young woman, green in this way, has penetrated through the eyes so deep within, that afterwards she's been slow to depart. There's great danger in a woman clothed in this colour: so my opinion is, you would do better to call off your hunt of the gentle green one.

85

DANTE TO CINO

Since I find no one here with whom to speak of the Lord to whom you and I are subject, I must satisfy the great longing I feel to express good thoughts in verse. Lay the

Null'altra cosa appo voi m'accagioni   5
del lungo e del noioso tacer mio
se non il loco ov'i' son, ch'è sì rio
che 'l ben non trova chi albergo li doni.

Donna non ci ha ch'Amor le venga al volto,
né omo ancora che per lui sospiri;   10
e chi 'l facesse qua sarebbe stolto.

Oh, messer Cin, come 'l tempo è rivolto
a danno nostro e de li nostri diri,
da po' che 'l ben è sì poco ricolto!

85*a* (B.XCVII)

RISPOSTA DI CINO

Dante, i' non so in qual albergo soni
lo ben, ch'è da ciascun messo in oblio:
è sì gran tempo che di qua fuggio
che del contraro son nati li troni;

e per le varïate condizioni   5
chi 'l ben tacesse, non risponde al fio:
lo ben sa' tu che predicava Iddio,
e nol tacea nel regno de' dimoni.

Dunque, s'al ben ciascun ostello è tolto
nel mondo, in ogni parte ove ti giri,   10
vuoli tu anco far dispiacer molto?

Diletto frate mio, di pene involto,
merzé, per quella donna che tu miri,
d'opra non star, se di fé non se' sciolto.

blame for my long, boorish silence on nothing but the place where I am, which is so evil that goodness finds no one to take it in.

There is no lady here such that Love would ever come into her face, nor any man who sighs for love—and whoever did so here would be a fool. O messer Cino, how the times are changed for the worse, for us and for our poetry, now that goodness finds such scanty welcome!

85a

CINO TO DANTE

Dante, I don't know in what dwelling goodness is heard, now that it is forgotten by all: it fled from here so long ago that the lightning of its contrary already flashes. Yet to keep silent about it because of the altered circumstances would be to fail in one's duty: you know that God proclaimed goodness openly, and did not stay silent even in the devils' kingdom.

So then, if goodness is robbed of shelter all over the world, wherever you turn, do you too wish to cause it great distress? My dear brother, surrounded by troubles as you are, I beg you, by that lady you contemplate, do not cease from works, if you've not lost faith.

86*a* (B.CX)

Dante, quando per caso s'abbandona
lo disio amoroso de la speme
che nascer fanno gli occhi del bel seme
di quel piacer che dentro si ragiona,

i' dico, poi se morte le perdona   5
e Amore tienla più de le due estreme,
che l'alma sola, la qual più non teme,
si può ben trasformar d'altra persona.

E ciò mi fa dir quella ch'è maestra
di tutte cose, per quel ch'i' sent'anco   10
entrato, lasso, per la mia fenestra.

Ma prima che m'uccida il nero e il bianco,
da te, che se' istato dentro ed extra,
vorre' saper se 'l mi' creder è manco.

86 (B.CXI)

RISPOSTA DI DANTE

Io sono stato con Amore insieme
da la circulazion del sol mia nona,
e so com'egli affrena e come sprona,
e come sotto lui si ride e geme.

Chi ragione o virtù contra gli sprieme,   5
fa come que' che 'n la tempesta sona,
credendo far colà dove si tona
esser le guerre de' vapori sceme.

86a

Dante, when by chance it happens that the love-desire despairs of that hope which the eyes cause to grow from the fair seed of beauty revolved in the mind, then I say that—if death reprieves her, and if Love controls her more than the two extremes—the soul, left to herself and fearing nothing more now, is fully at liberty to change to another person.

And I'm led to say this by her who is mistress in all things, because of him who I feel has entered once more, alas, at my window. But before the black and the white kill me, I should like to hear from you—who have been both inside and out—whether my opinion is ill founded.

86

I have been together with Love since my ninth revolution of the sun, and I know how he curbs and spurs, and how under his sway one laughs and groans. He who urges reason or virtue against him acts like one who raises his voice in a storm, thinking so to lessen the conflict of the clouds, there where the thunder rolls.

Però nel cerchio de la sua palestra
liber arbitrio già mai non fu franco,   10
sì che consiglio invan vi si balestra.

Ben può con nuovi spron punger lo fianco,
e qual che sia 'l piacer ch'ora n'addestra,
seguitar si convien, se l'altro è stanco.

87*a* (B. CXII)

MESSER CINO DA PISTOIA
AL MARCHESE MOROELLO MALASPINA

Cercando di trovar minera in oro
di quel valor cui gentilezza inchina,
punto m'ha 'l cor, marchese, mala spina,
in guisa che, versando il sangue, i' moro.

E più per quel ched i' non trovo ploro   5
che per la vita natural che fina:
cotal pianeta, lasso, mi destina
che dov'io perdo volentier dimoro.

E più le pene mie vi farie conte,
se non ched i' non vo' che troppa gioia   10
vo' concepiate di ciò che m'è noia.

Ben poria il mio segnor, anzi ch'io moia,
far convertir in oro duro monte,
c'ha fatto già di marmo nascer fonte.

87 (B. CXIII)

RISPOSTA DI DANTE
IN NOME DEL MARCHESE MOROELLO

Degno fa voi trovare ogni tesoro
la voce vostra sì dolce e latina,
ma volgibile cor ven disvicina,
ove stecco d'Amor mai non fé foro

Thus within his arena's bounds free will was never free, so that counsel looses its shafts in vain there. Love can indeed prick the flank with new spurs; and whatever the attraction may be that is now leading us, follow we must, if the other is outworn.

87a

CINO DA PISTOIA TO MARCHESE MOROELLO
MALASPINA

While I was seeking the gold-ore of that quality to which nobility of heart does homage, an evil thorn, Marquis, pierced my heart, so that I'm dying from loss of blood; but I weep for what I do not find rather than because my natural life is ending: such a planet, alas, controls my destiny that I willingly remain where I am the loser.

And I'd tell you more of my suffering except that I don't want you to get great enjoyment from what is distressing to me. Of course, my lord—who once made a spring gush forth from marble—could, before I die, change a rocky mountain into gold.

87

DANTE (ON BEHALF OF MOROELLO MALASPINA)
TO CINO

Your sweet and clear voice makes you worthy to find any treasure, but your fickle heart, where the barb of love never made a wound, leads you away from it. I who

Io che trafitto sono in ogni poro   5
del prun che con sospir si medicina,
pur trovo la minera in cui s'affina
quella virtù per cui mi discoloro.

Non è colpa del sol se l'orba fronte
nol vede quando scende e quando poia,   10
ma de la condizion malvagia e croia.

S'i' vi vedesse uscir de gli occhi ploia
per prova fare a le parole conte,
non mi porreste di sospetto in ponte.

88 (B. CXIV)

DANTE A MESSER CINO DA PISTOIA

Io mi credea del tutto esser partito
da queste nostre rime, messer Cino,
ché si conviene omai altro cammino
a la mia nave più lungi dal lito:

ma perch'i'ho di voi più volte udito   5
che pigliar vi lasciate a ogni uncino,
piacemi di prestare un pocolino
a questa penna lo stancato dito.

Chi s'innamora sì come voi fate,
or qua or là, e sé lega e dissolve,   10
mostra ch'Amor leggermente il saetti.

Però, se leggier cor così vi volve,
priego che con vertù il correggiate,
sì che s'accordi i fatti a' dolci detti.

am pierced at every pore by the thorn whose wound is treated with sighs, do nevertheless find the ore by which that power is refined through which I grow pale.

It is no fault of the sun if a blind face doesn't see him when he sets and rises, but of its evil, gross condition. If I were to see rain pour from your eyes to confirm the truth of your fine speech, you still would not put me in two minds as to my suspicion.

88

DANTE TO CINO

I thought, messer Cino, that I had quite abandoned this poetry of ours; for now my ship must hold a different course, being further from the shore. But since I have heard more than once that you let yourself be caught on every hook, I feel moved to put my tired fingers briefly to this pen.

One who falls in love as you do, now here, now there, and both binds and looses himself, shows that Love wounds him but lightly. So, if a fickle heart thus whirls you around, I beg you to correct it with virtue, so that your deeds accord with your sweet words.

88*a* (B. CXV)

Poi ch'i' fu', Dante, dal mio natal sito
fatto per greve essilio pellegrino
e lontanato dal piacer più fino
che mai formasse il Piacer infinito,

io son piangendo per lo mondo gito   5
sdegnato del morir come meschino;
e s'ho trovato a lui simil vicino,
dett'ho che questi m'ha lo cor ferito.

Né da le prime braccia dispietate,
onde 'l fermato disperar m'assolve,   10
son mosso perch'aiuto non aspetti;

ch'un piacer sempre me lega ed involve,
il qual conven che a simil di beltate
in molte donne sparte mi diletti.

89 (B. CXVI)

Amor, da che convien pur ch'io mi doglia
perché la gente m'oda,
e mostri me d'ogni vertute spento,
  dammi savere a pianger come voglia,
sì che 'l duol che si snoda   5
portin le mie parole com'io 'l sento.
  Tu vo' ch'io muoia, e io ne son contento:
ma chi mi scuserà, s'io non so dire
ciò che mi fai sentire?
chi crederà ch'io sia omai sì colto?   10
E se mi dai parlar quanto tormento,
fa', signor mio, che innanzi al mio morire
questa rëa per me nol possa udire:
ché, se intendesse ciò che dentro ascolto,
pietà faria men bello il suo bel volto.   15

88*a*

Dante, ever since harsh exile made me a wanderer from my birthplace and put a distance between me and the most exquisite beauty that ever the infinite Beauty fashioned, I have gone grieving about the world, a poor wretch disdained by death; but when I've found near me any beauty like to *that* one, I've said it was *this* one that wounded my heart.

Nor—though I expect no help—have I ever left those first pitiless arms from which a well-grounded despair releases me: for it is always one and the same beauty that binds and trammels me; and this perforce delights me in whatever is like it in beauty in many different women.

89

1. Love, since after all I am forced to grieve for others to hear me and to show myself bereft of all resistance, grant me the skill as well as the will to lament; so that the grief that is unleashed may be carried by my words just as I feel it. You wish me to die, and I am satisfied: but who will excuse me if I cannot put into words what you make me feel? Who will believe that I am now so in the power of another? But if you do give me speech to match my pain, see to it, my Lord, that this cruel woman may not hear it from me before I die; for, were she to hear what I listen to within, pity would make her fair face less fair.

Io non posso fuggir ch'ella non vegna
ne l'imagine mia,
se non come il pensier che la vi mena.
   L'anima folle, che al suo mal s'ingegna,
com'ella è bella e ria,   20
così dipinge, e forma la sua pena:
   poi la riguarda, e quando ella è ben piena
del gran disio che de li occhi le tira,
incontro a sé s'adira,
c'ha fatto il foco ond'ella trista incende.   25
Quale argomento di ragion raffrena,
ove tanta tempesta in me si gira?
L'angoscia, che non cape dentro, spira
fuor de la bocca sì ch'ella s'intende,
e anche a li occhi lor merito rende.   30

   La nimica figura, che rimane
vittorïosa e fera
e signoreggia la vertù che vole,
   vaga di se medesma andar mi fane
colà dov'ella è vera,   35
come simile a simil correr sòle.
   Ben conosco che va la neve al sole,
ma più non posso: fo come colui
che, nel podere altrui,
va co' suoi piedi al loco ov'egli è morto.   40
Quando son presso, parmi udir parole
dicer: 'Vie via vedrai morir costui!'
Allor mi volgo per veder a cui
mi raccomandi; e 'ntanto sono scorto
da li occhi che m'ancidono a gran torto.   45

2. I cannot avoid her coming into my imagination any more than the thought that brings her there. My rash soul, actively working to its own harm, depicts her there with all the beauty and malice that is hers, thus giving shape to its own torment: then it gazes at her so imaged, and when it is wholly filled with the great desire that it draws from her eyes, it falls into a rage against itself for having lit the fire in which it miserably burns. What rational argument has power to curb when such a tempest whirls within me? My anguish, which cannot be confined, pours out audibly in breath from the mouth and also gives my eyes what they deserve.

3. The hostile image, that remains victorious and pitiless and dominates the faculty of willing, attracted to herself, makes me go to where she is in reality, as like runs towards like. Well I know that it is snow going to the sun, but I can do nothing else: I'm as a man in another's power who goes on his own two feet to the place where he is killed. When I draw near her I seem to hear words that say: 'In a moment you will see him die!' Then I turn to see to whom I can have recourse, but in the same moment the eyes light on me which so unjustly slay me.

Qual io divegno sì feruto, Amore,
sailo tu, e non io,
che rimani a veder me sanza vita;
   e se l'anima torna poscia al core,
ignoranza ed oblio   50
stato è con lei, mentre ch'ella è partita.
   Com'io risurgo, e miro la ferita
che mi disfece quand'io fui percosso,
confortar non mi posso
sì ch'io non triemi tutto di paura.   55
E mostra poi la faccia scolorita
qual fu quel trono che mi giunse a dosso;
che se con dolce riso è stato mosso,
lunga fïata poi rimane oscura,
perché lo spirto non si rassicura.   60

   Così m'hai concio, Amore, in mezzo l'alpi,
ne la valle del fiume
lungo il qual sempre sopra me se' forte:
   qui vivo e morto, come vuoi, mi palpi,
merzé del fiero lume   65
che sfolgorando fa via a la morte.
   Lasso, non donne qui, non genti accorte
veggio, a cui mi lamenti del mio male:
se a costei non ne cale,
non spero mai d'altrui aver soccorso.   70
E questa sbandeggiata di tua corte,
signor, non cura colpo di tuo strale:
fatto ha d'orgoglio al petto schermo tale,
ch'ogni saetta lì spunta suo corso;
per che l'armato cor da nulla è morso.   75

4. What I become when so stricken, you know, Love, not I—you who stay to see me lifeless. And though in time the soul returns to my heart, nescience and oblivion were with it all the time it was away. When I get to my feet and gaze at the wound that destroyed me when I received the blow, I cannot so take heart as not to tremble all over with fear. And then my face, drained of its colour, shows what that lightning was which struck me; for though the lightning flashed from a lovely smile, my face remains darkened for a long while after, because my spirit does not regain courage.

5. To this state, Love, you have reduced me, among the mountains, in that river's valley along whose banks you have always been powerful over me: here, just as you will, you knead me, both alive and dead, thanks to that pitiless light which with a lightning flash opens the way for death. Alas, here I see no ladies, no person of sensitive mind with whom to lament of my plight. If this woman does not care, I can never hope for help from others; and this outlaw from your court, my Lord, is heedless of your arrows, for she has made a breastplate of disdain such that every arrow blunts its flight there, and nothing bites through to her heart within its armour.

O montanina mia canzon, tu vai:
forse vedrai Fiorenza, la mia terra,
che fuor di sé mi serra,
vota d'amore e nuda di pietate;
se dentro v'entri, va' dicendo: 'Omai   80
non vi può far lo mio fattor più guerra:
là ond'io vegno una catena il serra
tal, che se piega vostra crudeltate,
non ha di ritornar qui libertate'.

My mountain song, go your way. Perhaps you will see Florence, my city, that shuts me out from her, void of love and stripped of compassion. If you should enter, say: 'Now my maker can make war on you no longer: he's bound by such a chain in the place I come from that even were your harshness to relax, he is not free to return here.'

COMPARATIVE TABLE OF BARBI'S NUMBERING OF THE POEMS

Barbi	Foster–Boyde	Barbi	Foster–Boyde	Barbi	Foster–Boyde
I	6	XL	1	LXXIX	59
II	6a	XLI	2	LXXX	60
III	6b	XLII	2a	LXXXI	61
IV	6c	XLIII	3	LXXXII	69
V	10	XLIV	3a	LXXXIII	70
VI	11	XLV	4	LXXXIV	62
VII	12	XLVI	5a	LXXXV	63
VIII	20	XLVII	5	LXXXVI	71
IX	24	XLVIII	8	LXXXVII	64
X	26	XLIX	9	LXXXVIII	65
XI	27	L	13	LXXXIX	66
XII	28	LI	14	XC	67
XIII	29	LII	15	XCI	68
XIV	33	LIII	15a	XCII	75a
XV	—	LIV	—	XCIII	75
XVI	34	LV	—	XCIV	84a
XVII	35	LVI	21	XCV	84
XVIII	36	LVII	22	XCVI	85
XIX	37	LVIII	23	XCVII	85a
XX	40	LIX	17	XCVIII	—
XXI	42	LX	18	XCIX	76
XXII	43	LXI	16	C	77
XXIII	44	LXII	7	CI	78
XXIV	46	LXIII	19	CII	79
XXV	47	LXIV	—	CIII	80
XXVI	48	LXV	30	CIV	81
XXVII	49	LXVI	31	CV	82
XXVIII	—	LXVII	32	CVI	83
XXIX	—	LXVIII	25	CVII	—
XXX	50	LXIX	45	CVIII	—
XXXI	51	LXX	38	CIX	—
XXXII	52	LXXI	39	CX	86a
XXXIII	53	LXXII	41	CXI	86
XXXIV	54	LXXIII	72	CXII	87a
XXXV	55	LXXIV	72a	CXIII	87
XXXVI	56	LXXV	73	CXIV	88
XXXVII	57	LXXVI	73a	CXV	88a
XXXVIII	57a	LXXVII	74	CXVI	89
XXXIX	1a	LXXVIII	74a	CXVII	58

INDEX OF FIRST LINES

INDEX TO FIRST LINES

PRINTED IN GREAT BRITAIN
AT THE UNIVERSITY PRESS, OXFORD
BY VIVIAN RIDLER
PRINTER TO THE UNIVERSITY